D0861977

Lies of a Real Housewife

[TELL THE TRUTH AND SHAME THE DEVIL]

A MEMOIR

ANGELA STANTON

FOREWORD BY **DR. ALVEDA KING**

© 2012 Angela Stanton
ISBN: 978-19358836-3-0

Written by Angela Stanton
Edited by Anthony Whyte
Design & Photography by Jason Claiborne

All rights reserved. No parts of this book may be used or reproduced in any manner whatsoever
without written permission, except in the case of brief quotations embodied in critical articles and
reviews. For further information contact Augustus Publishing

WHERE
**HIP HOP
LITERATURE**
BEGINS...

Augustus Publishing paperback November 2012
www.augustuspublishing.com

"The man of integrity walks securely, but he who takes the crooked path will be found out."

PROVERBS 10:9 (NIV)

Acknowledgements

I thank my Father in heaven for His most gracious mercy. All things are possible through Christ.

To my mother, Joan Milling, your works were not in vain. My husband who is truly God sent; my brother Lee, my children, and my faith kept me while on this journey. Dr. Alveda King, Shayla Thompson, Michelle Uchiama, Paula Britt, Anthony Whyte, and Rosy Stefanatos thank you, and everyone who believed in me. I even thank those

who didn't believe. Your hurdles only made me jump higher!

To all my special friends, the ones who stand behind the curtains, because you all have blessed me; I am now in a position to bless and touch the lives of so many others. It's the gift that keeps on giving.

Without you all this would have never been possible.

Angela Stanton

Introduction

Murderers, pimps, prostitutes, hustlers, drug dealers, scammers and con artists all have their place in this world. It's not what you have done in your past if you learned from your mistakes, it's what you're doing to make this world a better place. I don't have the slightest idea what you or anyone else reading this book may think of me. After reading my words, many of you may feel that people who have committed crimes don't deserve a second chance.

I've got news for you. We all play our role in society. Without crime there would be no cops, no lawyers, no judges, no prisons, no police stations, and more importantly, no justice system. I think you understand where I am going with this. Like it or not, criminals employ half of the country. The sad part about all of this is that in order for someone to do right—someone has to do wrong.

Foreword

Lies of a Real Housewife is a journey, the telling of make or break life experiences, the kind that could either kill you or make you stronger. Someone once said, "If at first you don't succeed, give the orange a bigger squeeze." Another said, "If life gives you a lemon, make lemonade." Well, Angela Stanton has the courage to squeeze hard, and to sweeten the bitterness by telling the truth.

A favorite scripture asks, "Have I become your enemy because I tell you the truth?" Some may read this book and wonder how some of the many people Angela met on her journey could even dream of getting away with the acts described herein? The book may cause some to wonder, how can all of this be true? Well, the truth is in the telling.

Angela Stanton does not pretend to be perfect. She doesn't hide her pain behind veils of celebrity glamour and make-believe, goodie-two-shoes scenarios.

Lies of a Real Housewife is the telling of a series of events, leading to the crumbling of a house of cards. The author is on a quest for inner healing. The book is also an effort to reveal that there is more to life than often meets the eye.

We all know of situations where we have been betrayed by someone

close to us. Such a person may come in the guise of friend and helper. Then turns the table and becomes our worst nightmare. Many of us have suffered through this, and worse, but it's what we chose to do about the betrayal inside us that counts.

There is another saying, "Tell the truth and shame the devil." Angela Stanton is not out to get back at anyone. We're all victim of our own duplicities. Actually, Angela would like to see us all become liberated from what has been crafted by Lies of a Real Housewife.

It has been said that there is good in everyone. It has also been said that everyone has the potential to do things that they wish they wouldn't do. Angela lives in an imperfect world, where things aren't always what they seem to be. She searches for not only a better life but also recovery in her life. This is a story of how the life of a five-year-old who was sexually abused unraveled, and what happened on her journey to find redemption.

Dr. Alveda King

Preface

I remember waking up and walking down this long hallway to go to the bathroom. When I got inside the bathroom, I closed the door then I turned on the light. To my surprise, my older cousin, Dee, was inside the bathroom hiding behind the door! I was more shocked than scared. Daddy taught me never to be afraid of anything. But what happened next frightened me. Dee was fifteen years old, and I was only five years. He pulled up my nightgown and started digging his fingers into my vagina area. While covering my mouth, my cousin tried to shove his penis between my lips. I didn't know what he wanted me to do, so he started punching me on the side of my head. Dee let me go after he was fully satisfied. I ran out of the bathroom and down the long hallway. Then I jumped into the bed with my younger cousin. I wrapped myself tightly in the covers. I was terrified, and didn't want him to get me again. My mind was racing, and I was crying for my daddy. He was far away and couldn't hear me. Finally, I cried myself to sleep.

That morning when I awoke, I kept telling my grandmother, Shug, I wanted to go home. I begged her to call my daddy, but she was concerned about running up her phone bill. I was afraid.

Angela 4 years old,
seven months before
she got molested

Angela 5 years old,
one month after her
molestation took place

Betrayal can be very painful, but when the person who betrays you is a family member or someone you consider a close friend, then the pain is always on a totally different level.

Phaedra Parks was a snake I allowed to slither her way into my life. Once she got close enough to bite, she did! As she slithered away, she left me to die a slow and sure death. The heifer never even looked back.

As I replay the course of our relationship in my mind over and over again, I think of all the times she visited my mother's and my grandmother's home then sat down, removed her shoes, and ate a meal. I remember the times she played with my children. I've replayed each and every moment that I spent with her! The laughter, the heartfelt tears, the times when I was going through a beat down and stressed out from the blows thrown by life; she was my true confidante.

Phaedra Parks was even bold enough to stand in my absence at my very own mother's funeral! I know your mind is wondering where I was, and why I was not there myself. Well, believe it or not, I was incarcerated at Pulaski State Prison serving "OUR" sentence!

So here it is– within the first six months of my incarceration, I gave birth to my fifth child while handcuffed to a bed. My mother died suddenly of a massive heart attack, and my grandmother died as well. They always say, "God won't put more on you than you can bear!" Well, if I may be frank... I think that was a bit much for anybody to bear.

Sometimes our world can be a very cruel place, nothing in my life had prepared me for the journey I was about to take. Looking back now I know that I only made it by the grace and mercy of my Heavenly father. Brace yourself as I take you on the ride of your life. The biggest emotional roller coaster you will have ever experienced. On this ride you will experience love, betrayal, happiness, hate, shame, guilt, defeat, fear, and last but certainly not least, VICTORY!

Phaedra Parks is very calculative. She's a smart woman. I will give her that credit. She walked away from our treasured turned corrupt friendship with not as much as a blemish to her name. To top that, she carried her secret around long enough for the statute of limitations to run out on any criminal or civil charges. She even married our partner in crime so that he could not ever testify against her, but have you ever heard the saying, "You're so smart that you're dumb?" This statement was most certainly created for Phaedra Parks. Sorry, but that good ol' Christian girl--that southern belle is a crook. And she's a dumb one at that!

This is a true story of my life, and my personal relationship with re-nowned 'super lawyer' Phaedra Parks. This is the truth behind those lies.

Chapter One
The Path to Destruction

"Enter through the narrow gate. For wide is the gate and broad is the road that leads to destruction, and many enter through it."

Matthew 7:13 (NIV)

I was born in Baltimore, Maryland, and grew up a hardhead, a real hard-knocker in Buffalo, NY. I wasn't afraid of anything or anybody because I was raised on the streets during the 1980's. When I was five years old, I was sexually abused by a monster. The perverted culprit was my mother's nephew, Anthony, who was several years older than me. This horrendous incident left me in a state of desperation. In my first book, Life Beyond These Walls, I eventually wrote an in-depth perspective of this brutal attack. and the cruelty perpetrated against me. I left an excerpt of my first book in the back of this book.

After surviving the grisly sex abuse episode at the tender age of five, I gained the notoriety of being the black sheep of my family. My dire circumstance pushed me over the brink of early disaster, and landed me in the worst years of my childhood. It propelled me into being an angry, young girl who was constantly in and out of trouble.

At the time, I didn't know that the silent, inner conflict I bore would

leave me scarred for life. I found myself always fighting for, and always demanding attention from anyone. On a daily basis, my poor mother, Joan Milling, could've bet her life that she would receive a call from a representative of whatever school I was attending. And that was when I attended school. My mother would've been a millionaire if she got twenty dollars for every call she received.

Yes, the sexual abuse I suffered pushed me into being a most disruptive child. I felt that classmates and children in general were always picking on me all the time. It had partly to do with me being physically so tall. My mother was five-feet-nine inches tall, my father, Ronnie was six-feet-five inches, and my brother, Lee Matthews, was six-feet-seven inches tall.

To make matters worse, I had allergies, and always had a runny nose. My kindergarten teacher got mad with me one day because she felt I was disrupting her class when I asked for tissue. But I had actually sneezed, and snot was everywhere. She angrily grabbed me by my shirt, dragged me to the side of the classroom, and shouted, "You snotty-nose brat, bring your own damn tissue next time!"

All the kids started calling me 'snot-nose brat'. They wouldn't stop, so I was always in a fight. I mean, this was happening all the time! When I first told my mother that I was molested by her sister's third son, my family chose to sweep it under the rug. This was done to maintain the strong bond of kinship. But it served only to destroy my trust, and made me a fighter. I felt if my mother would no longer protect me then who would? I had low self esteem and suffered intolerable depression. Then to top it off, I had grown an insatiable obsession for sex.

The fact that I had been through the horrible ordeal of molestation didn't help me or my family any. This heinous act fueled my deviant behavior and made it difficult for my mother to maintain a decent job. I hated when they called her to my school because I would always get yelled at.

"Angela, one day your mouth is going to write a check that your butt can't cash! G-i-i-r-r-l-l-l! You are going to find yourself in a world of trouble one day!" My mother used to say. I can still hear my mother's voice replaying over and over again. Her words continue to always echo somewhere in the back of my mind.

I attended over eleven schools before I was finally kicked out permanently. Then I was sent to an alternative school, and was expelled from there as well. Night school became my next stop. And guess what? The result was the same. I was expelled from there too.

Six weeks later my mother received a letter stating I would not be allowed to attend any schools in New York State. This was disappointing to me. I felt like yesterday's garbage, nobody wanted me. But I was a naive child whose innocence had been taken away. I had been robbed of a pain-free childhood. As a result I would be labeled a 'troubled child'. This was the description of my shrink, the psychiatrist, placed in charge of evaluating how troubled I really was when I was nine years old.

To others I was just rude, or disrespectful. There were some, who saw me as a defiant, belligerent, and disorderly child. Then some people wrote me off as being uncontrollable, nasty, mean-spirited, and possessed. I was a demon, or just plain full of hate. You could call it whatever you want, but I knew that I was just always misunderstood. Deep down inside I was mad that I wasn't important enough for my mother to stand up for me.

Totally out of control, I was no stranger to counseling and detention centers. I hated listening to the repetitive cycle of questioning from the counselors. Their curiosities always wound up being compounded into the shape of the same questions.

"Angela, what's wrong? Angela, why are you acting out? What happened to you honey? How can I help…?"

It all just sounded like blah, blah, blah to me! And I hated listening to them because I knew they really didn't care. There was no bond. So I never had a connection with any of them, and never felt the urge to want to really open up. All I wanted to know was why were they in my face with that nonsense? I really knew they were being fake, acting like they really cared about me.

What really bothered me the most was that everyone, including the counselors, would always claim to know what was troubling me. If they knew what I was going through, then they should have been more sympathetic to my needs. They all should have been more understanding, but they didn't know how it felt to have innocence stolen at such a tender age.

At five years old, I should have been enjoying my childhood, looking forward to happy meals at McDonalds, and rushing home to watch Sesame Street. The only butterflies I should have felt in my stomach should have been those of my excitement to see Santa Claus. Instead I was molested.

I was under the impression that parents were supposed to protect their children. They should believe when their children say something bad happened. I didn't have that luxury. The dilemma made me wish that everyone would just get out of my face! My mother did nothing because a family member was the perpetrator. Then my grandmother had told her to keep the incident hush, hush and on the low.

My older brother, Lee, would tell you that I was a complete jerk back then. The truth was I felt no one really cared about me. The counselors could care less what happened to me, and providing therapy was just a job to them. Once that 'closed' sign was hung on the door, I was back out on the mean streets by myself, struggling. The counselors would be at their homes, in their perfect world with a perfect dinner table setting, kissing, and hugging their perfect children.

My poor mother, she didn't know what to do with me. I remembered when I was fourteen years old, and she learned that her baby-girl was pregnant. She was so disappointed and tried really hard to help me turn my life around. My mother even put me in a pregnancy crisis center for troubled girls.

I was kicked out three days later, after I got caught trying to steal the

sonogram machine. My mama refused to give up on me. She was determined that I was going to get my education. She never stopped stressing the fact that I needed to achieve more in life than being a juvenile delinquent. I was a teenage mother, and a high school dropout, but my mother stayed on my side. She always wanted what was best for me, and she was serious about that.

In 1994 she packed up everything that she could fit in the back of her vehicle, and we headed south. We both put Buffalo, N.Y. in our rearview mirrors. I never looked back because I knew the only things I was leaving behind me were all the bad memories of my childhood. I wanted to distance myself from that. Honestly, I was glad I made it out alive.

After driving for hours, we finally arrived at our destination. We put our roots down in Greensboro, North Carolina. My mother wanted to move closer to her family in Atlanta, but not too near. She was the seventh child out of ten children, and yes, some were very dysfunctional.

The scenery was much different from what I had imagined. It was more laid-back and peaceful. I had heard stories about the south, but there was nothing like witnessing it in person. You could actually see the beautiful greenery. To me, this was something very foreign. I would often be stunned by the comparison to the broken concrete, and abandoned buildings I'd grown up around during my early childhood.

Everything just appeared to move so darn slow. The people of North

Carolina even talked, and moved at a slower pace. Buses and cars didn't go flying by. Everybody there seemed to be compassionate and caring. This was amazing to me and was like a breath of fresh air. I remember thinking I could learn to really like this place. Hope suddenly returned and positive thoughts started to fill my psyche. Maybe I could go to school, get a part-time job, and take care of my baby-girl, Aleea. I put a plan together and started doing exactly that. Then all hell broke loose!

But I'm moving real fast here. So let's take some time and return to a couple of years in my past life of horror in Buffalo. It was 1991 and my mother had met a man. She fell hard for him. He was a con artist and a scammer who went by the name of Curtis. As you already guess by now, I hated Curtis. From the beginning, I knew he was not right. But hey, what do you tell a person blinded by love?

By this time, my brother had graduated high school, and was upstate New York. Having received a scholarship for his athletic talents, Lee was living his dream of playing basketball at Sienna College and my mother couldn't be prouder. Her son had made it out of Buffalo, and all she had to worry about was me. Lee eventually played basketball for Sienna College from 1988 to 1992. I was sure that he would never have approved of Curtis, and I actually couldn't wait for the day when they would meet.

Before meeting Curtis, my mother had already made a name for herself. She was a very successful woman who was working in her field of choice. Joan Milling was an ambitious black woman with an entrepreneurial

spirit who owned her own successful business. With nothing more than her faith, she had established a successful real estate business from scratch.

We were not by any means filthy rich, but were definitely not poor. If I had only learn to follow the rules, I could've had my heart's desires. But I was rebellious, and breaking rules became a bad habit. I didn't feel it was in my DNA to follow or be confined by anyone's rules.

Curtis was a homebuilder who wanted to start his own construction company, and saw my mother as an opportunity for his selfish gains. In her real estate business, she would purchase abandoned homes, and he was hired to renovate them. Well, that was the initial plan. The second time in my life I ever laid my eyes on Curtis, he was introduced to me as my step-father. My blood instantly began boiling at the thought of this man being anything significant in my life.

Things immediately started to change the moment Curtis moved into our home. My brother, Lee was seven hours away, and was absolutely clueless to the recent change of events. He was spared the experience of living with the homewrecker known as Curtis.

My mother began asking this man for permission to speak. This was a strong indication to me that something was amiss. Anyone who knew my mother would tell you how outspoken she was. Joan Milling was always known for being a leader. She was headstrong, honest, and smart. There was power in her voice, but soon it would all be silenced. And this happened whenever Curtis walked into the room.

I could hear them fighting at nights when she would leave me in the living room watching my favorite TV show. She would be in her bedroom, and I could hear him beating my mother. On one occasion, I remember sitting in the living room with two of my childhood friends. Out of nowhere, my mother came running and screaming for dear life. Following right behind her, chasing my naked mother with a knife was sorry-ass Curtis. I immediately jumped up, ran into the kitchen, and grabbed the biggest knife I could find. Then I took off after him.

By the time I made it outside, I could see my mother running barefooted through the cold, icy street which was covered with snow. Curtis jumped in his car, and he was actually attempting to run my mother down. Luckily, she made it back to the house, locked all the doors, and immediately called the police.

The next morning, she took out a restraining order against Curtis. But later that day, this evil man returned to our home and cut all the electrical wires to the house. It took the National Grid power company five days to repair the lines. During this time, my mother and I were prisoners in our own home. We remained trapped without electricity while the awful smell of rotting food filled our nostrils for days. This occurred because my mother was too frightened to leave the house. On the other hand, I refused to be a captive in my own home.

My mind was already made up. I made a promise to myself that I would kill this creep. My mother knew it too. She was not only aware of my

plan to commit murder, but she felt it! In this harsh world, we were all each other had. There was no way I was going to stand by and let this con man take my mother away from me.

I already hated life and the only thing I had left to lose was my mother. I wasn't having that, so my blade was persistently by my side. I slept with it each and every night. Patiently, I waited to seek my revenge exclusively on the man who beat my dear mother.

To my dismay, a couple of days later, they were back together like nothing had happened. I couldn't understand this development, and needless to say, I wasn't just angry, but I was very frustrated. I had reached the limit of my boiling point. Unable to fathom my mother's actions, I moved out of the house. This time it was for good. I had had it at this point.

Surviving by any means necessary, I lived on the streets of Buffalo. I hated my mother's husband, and he hated me. There was absolutely no way that we were going to exist under the same roof. Where could I stay to get off the streets? I was a teenage girl. My options were limited, and few. I definitely was not, and could not live with my natural father.

His wife would not allow it. She hated my mother the most. There was no option, but to extend her hatred in my direction. My mother gave him something she couldn't, and my mother had something she didn't. I was his only child! But why did she hate me? I did not ask those two people to have sex, and bring a life into this world! I resembled my mother. And to this very day, my father's wife still harbors a strong revulsion toward me.

Every other day I would stop by and check in on my mother. I wanted to see how she was doing, and to learn what the wacko had up his sleeves. My mother was kind enough to give me a job in her office. This kept me out of trouble, and she paid me pretty good too. My mother taught me office management, how to create files, make copies, fax papers, and read good faith estimates. She spoke to me a lot less, and I could tell that something was bothering her. I just didn't know what it was.

One day, after having a quiet mother and daughter lunch, we returned to her office. A tall man with a thin build, accompanied by a petite woman with red hair, who I later learned was his wife, showed up at the office. The man was loud and adamant about needing to speak with my mother right away. She directed the couple down the hall to her office, and closed the door.

Like any inquisitive child, I made sure I got close enough where I could hear every single word. I overheard the ranting of the irate man. He was threatening my mother. He told her that if she did not have his money in thirty days, he would have her arrested. Then he grabbed his wife by the hand, and together they stormed out.

My heart raced erratically. The thought of my mother going to jail was extremely terrifying to me. I heard her on the phone arguing with someone from her bank. Thousands of dollars were missing from her business escrow account. No money had been removed from her personal account, but the money earmarked for her real estate clients was gone.

The next few weeks were like something out of a nightmare. My mother was avoiding telephone calls, telling people she wasn't there while being in her office. Then she began eyeing everyone around her as if they were suspects in a plot against her. She had even put me—her only daughter, the one she gave birth to, at a distance. After a couple of weeks passed, a friend of mine handed me a newspaper, and told me to read it. Right there on the newspaper's front page was a picture of my mother, her home, and her business. She had been charged with fraud, and the federal agents had seized everything she owned.

Her whole escrow account, amounting to eighty-thousand dollars had been wiped out. Curtis had gotten my mother real good. My entire child-hood I watched her work hard, and made innumerable sacrifices in order to build a successful business. Then Curtis came along, and stole it all away from right under her nose. So packing up everything and moving to Greens-boro, North Carolina, was a welcomed change. Both me and my mother were overdue a fresh start.

Living in Greensboro initially proved to be a great idea. My mother went back to working hard in an attempt to rebuild her life. I was working part time as a waitress, and going to school in the evenings for my G.E.D. I loved my new life. Nobody knew me or my mother in North Carolina, and nobody pointed a finger at us or gave us any type of suspicious looks. The people were warm and treated us with respect. We got along with them and blended in just fine.

The bittersweet parody of my new situation was confounding to me. There was a rebellion going on inside my head, and it turned me into the type of person who couldn't stand being told what to do. Working as a waitress proved to be both challenging and stressful. I detested taking orders from anyone, including my own parents. I hated manual labor. I was young and in great shape, but the only place I wanted to stand on my feet for eight hours or better was at the nightclub. After work, I walked three and a half miles each day to get home. Once I made it home the first thing on my list was to fix a cold drink. I would kick off my shoes, and check on my mother. Then see how my baby girl, Aleea, was doing.

After my usual rough day at work, this was one of my favorite times of the day. This day, however would prove to be different. I saw my mother's purse on the kitchen counter, but a quick glance made me realize that she wasn't around. I went into my bedroom and noticed Aleea alone on my bed. She was asleep. This was very unusual. My mother was in love with Aleea, and the only time she left Aleea's side was when she had to go to work.

I immediately spun around and walked toward my mother's bedroom door. Finding her door closed came as a huge surprise to me. I kept turning the doorknob, to no avail. Frantically, I started to knock, which amounted to me banging on the door. There was still no answer.

Thinking of all the horrid possibilities, my thoughts spurred my ac-

tions into a more urgent state. Fearing the worst, I really began to worry at this point. I hurried back to the kitchen, and grabbed a butter knife to jimmy the locked door. I popped the bolt off my mother's door, and was not at all prepared for what came next.

Curtis! That bastard was chilling in my mother's bed. His feet kicked up, a cigarette was dangling from the side of his mouth. He had that ugly smirk on his lips. I hated that expression so much. The one that said, "Ah ha, I'm back. I run things now bi*ch!"

Oh my God! I thought. My breath was now coming in gasps and before I knew it, I couldn't breathe! I was searching, panting for air that disappeared from my surrounding like a flash of light. My vision became blurry and I felt the room spinning. Suddenly my throat was parched and I was getting very dizzy. Overwhelmed with confusion, the anxiety left my mind in a whirl. Questions still lingered in my baffled cranium. What the hell was Curtis doing here? I thought we had left him hundreds of miles back in the past behind us. How did he find us?

At the sight of this wicked man, I became so emotional that I found myself suddenly sprawled across my mother's bedroom floor. I collapsed as my mind couldn't take the shock. I passed out. Then I ended up in the emergency room, suffering a panic attack.

I remember lying in the bed at Wesley Long Community Hospital, looking around in astonishment, wishing, hoping, and praying that it was all a dream. There were doctors standing over me, pricking me in different places on my body attempting to resuscitate me. All I was able to think about was why would my mother let him come back?

This man had stolen her money, and robbed her of her dreams. Not only that, but he took away the plans she had for her children. Just when my mother and I had been getting along really good, reestablishing our lives, the home-wrecker reappeared. I wasn't getting into any kind of trouble, and I had been helping her with the bills. Why did she need him, and not me?

I sat up in the hospital bed, disconnected all the machines and wires from my body. Then I discharged myself. I did not know anyone in Greensboro. So it wasn't like I could just go somewhere for a couple of days. This time I had a child to think of and I had to make some real plans. Atlanta, Georgia was where my closest family resided. It was four hours away. Getting there was going to be a major problem.

My mother had to be crazy, crazy enough to let this crazy man back into her life. She was foolish to believe that I would feel right being anywhere close to him. I felt that my mother was doing as she pleased with no consideration of my feelings. I had to make a decision for me and Aleea.

So I put my plan into action. The first thing I did was call my natural father, Robert Stanton, who was home back in Buffalo, NY. I informed him of my plans. He pleaded with me to give him temporary custody of my daughter until I could get my life together. My current situation was unstable, and I knew that to be true. I loved my baby girl, and I swear to God that I did not want to let her go. She was so beautiful and innocent. My baby girl had

her whole life ahead of her. She did not deserve to be out on the streets. My life wasn't together. I was headed to Atlanta, but had no money. There was nowhere to live and I had no immediate direction. The last thing I wanted was for Aleea to grow up to be anything like me.

My father met me the next day. He was there to take Aleea back home to Buffalo, NY where she would reside with him and his wife. There was so much sadness in my actions as I began putting my baby in the back of my father's car. I packed her bag and her favorite toys in the trunk of the car then broke down in tears. Aleea was crying as well. She could care less if my situation was dire and unfit, she did not want to leave me. My baby loved me! I stood there numb, watching my father's car drive away. Holding my aching stomach, I saw how my firstborn was frantically kicking, trying to get out of her car seat. Then slowly the car disappeared out of view, and I went back inside. Through teary eyes, I kept looking through the peephole of the front door. I hated my life at that point.

With my daughter safely with my father, I had only myself to worry about. I packed my very few belongings, and began my journey to Atlanta, Georgia. The city was only four hours away and this was a relatively short trip. Little did I know the place would have brought many people, both good and bad, crossing my path. My actions would have life-changing, unforeseen consequences in the development of my adult life.

Now let me tell you about my relationship with Phaedra Parks, and the truth behind her deceitful web of lies. A lawyer who was very instrumental in my life, Phaedra helped me to realize that the one thing about lawyers we all know to be true was that they were great liars.

Chapter Two
The Devil in Disguise

*"Watch out for false prophets. They come to you in sheep's
clothing, but inwardly they are ferocious wolves."*

Matthew 7:15 (NIV)

My cousin, Kate, came up from Atlanta on a Greyhound. It was dark
and about two in the morning. We were able to 'illegally borrow' a neighbor's
Chevy Blazer. Kate's father was a good mechanic and had taught her everything about cars, including how to hotwire one. The passenger window was
broken out, but there was a full tank of gas. Sharing driving duties between
the two of us, we were able to make it down to Atlanta, Georgia.

When we arrived in Atlanta, I got a glimpse of how poor my family
in Georgia lived. That meant limited resources, and no handouts to anyone.
It was everyman for himself. There was one place for me to live. It was 306
Ormond Street. The house was located in an area of Atlanta called Summer
Hill. The house was home, not only to me, but to my entire extended maternal
family.

In the Fall of 1995, I started getting reacquainted with family members, and started hanging-out with my cousins. I hadn't seen Scott, Kate, Nikki and Cookie since I was seven years old. We were all around the same age, eighteen years old, give or take a few months. It was a happy homecoming. Nikki, Cookie, and I had always shared a certain bond. Being victims of similar abuse by the same molester, we were all trapped in the same nightmare.

If they were asked, my cousins would probably say that I was lucky because I got away. I didn't grow up in the same home with the predator, while they, on the other hand, didn't have a choice. One of my female cousins told me that one of my aunts caught the predator greasing her up in the hallway. He had a whole jar of Vaseline, and was applying a thick coat over her anus. This sick man was prepping her to be sodomized.

On hearing my aunt's footsteps coming down the hall, he dropped the Vaseline, and ran toward her shouting, "Look at what this nasty little girl is in here doing!" Enraged by the fact that she caught my cousin with her pants down, my aunt, without even giving her so much as a chance to explain, summarily beat my cousin like the poor girl had stolen the family heirloom.

Maybe in the eyes of my cousins I was lucky, but for me I lived with the awful memories. Even though I tried desperately to bury them in the past, like a bad tattoo, they resurfaced and still remained a part of me. I was thin skinned and sensitive. Every time the thought came to my mind, the bad memories would bring the abuse back to life.

In 1996 my mother had her fill of Curtis, and she moved to Atlanta.

She was ready to move on with her life. I was sitting on my grandmother's front porch when she pulled up in her 1991 white Lincoln Continental. All her belongings were in the trunk and the backseat of her car. She made the announcement that she was home for good, and for me, it turned into the happiest of homecomings. I had been on my own for a while now and needed the support of my mother. Even though I appeared to be as tough as nails on the outside, the inside was soft as pudding.

By now, I had been in Atlanta for just under a year. It was very difficult to make ends meet. Every friend, boyfriend, and pal I had, was into something illegal. Hotlanta was the name of this place. Everybody had some type of illicit hustle scheme going down. Where I lived, the motto was 'hustle or be hustled'. My cousins and I lived for the excitement of the nightlife Atlanta had to offer. Freedom and independence were new concepts to us. We didn't have to go to school, and didn't have to answer to our parents. It was all about enjoying our lives.

I was nineteen years old when Cookie and I decided to go out. The Bank Head Bounce was one of the hottest clubs in Atlanta at the time. I will never forget that night because it would be the beginning of an exciting but dangerous journey. That night I met Drama. Cookie and I had been in the club the whole night. We watched and enjoyed his performance on stage. On the way out of the club, I caught his eye, and he quickly made his way over to me. It was the beginning of our on-again, off-again romantic relationship.

Terrance Cook went by the moniker, Drama. He had a hit single

back then called, "Left, Right, Left." Drama was a knucklehead of a rapper, and couldn't stay out of trouble. Raheem the Dream had signed him to a record deal when Drama was still an underage teen.

This was where Phaedra Parks entered his music career, fighting for Drama's money. In the midst of Phaedra Parks suing Raheem the Dream for Drama's money, Drama got himself arrested for armed robbery. I never really heard anything else about that lawsuit, and I don't believe Drama ever saw a dime.

Between late 1998 and early 1999, Drama and I were in a relationship together. It was through my close connection with him that I would finally become acquainted with his high-powered attorney, Phaedra Parks. She not only talked the talk, but dressed from heels to head in all the latest fashions, she walked the walk. If she wasn't driving her black Benz then she was peeling off in her white Jaguar. Everybody in and around the city knew who Phaedra Parks was. When her designer heels walked into any room, she carried a certain light about her which shone and lit up the entire place.

Phaedra Parks was a fancy entertainment lawyer who appeared to be well accomplished. I had no idea that this was all smokescreens and mirrors. For the most part, her act was all part of a bigger deception. She was very impressive, driving around town in her black Mercedes Benz, and turning heads wherever she went.

Drama had everything going for him. He was at the height of his career, and just like the majority of rappers who allow drugs and crime to take over their lives, Drama was not different. Eventually, he was sentenced to twelve years in Clayton County, Georgia, for armed robbery.

I wasn't Drama's main chick, and was always in competition with many of his groupies. I was just one of his sidepieces, a jump-off, some may say. I don't mind admitting to that. Being molested at a young age infected me with the capacity to have relationships with men and not get emotionally attached. I was young and promiscuous. Drama was not the only man I was dating. I wasn't really concerned about being in a relationship with anyone at that time.

After meeting Phaedra Parks, she and I hit it off from the start for some reason. I would often wonder what kind of synergy bonded us together like glue. Whatever it was, it was a strong connection. Phaedra was like my big sister and helped to shape me into the person I grew into being. She had the answer to everything.

I was a girl who had been in and out of trouble my entire life. Being from a broken home, I was also silently suffering from being a victim of childhood sexual abuse. Phaedra was the exact opposite. She had the perfect upbringing. After attending and graduating from law school, she became a successful lawyer. As a young girl, I had always dreamt of being a lawyer. Phaedra was my mentor, and not only did I respect her, but I really admired her. She was like the princess in a fairytale book I had read as a child. Phaedra Parks was, in essence, the first positive female role model I had in my life besides my mother.

It lifted my spirit and revived hope inside me to have a friend who knew exactly where I wanted to be in life. Phaedra Parks had the resources to help me get there. I saw her as someone who could show me how to stay out of trouble, point me in the right direction, and help me straighten out my life. Phaedra showed me that there was much more to life than what I had seen. To be honest, Phaedra was my inspiration. For some reason I believed that she was somewhat my redeemer. At least that was what I thought.

Phaedra and I were very close. Her home was like a second home to me. She was always welcomed when she showed up at my grandmother's house. She won the approval of my grandmother. Every time Phaedra would stop by, she brought ticket loads of Scratch Off and a bottle of Smirnoff Vodka. That was all it took for my grandmother, Shug, to like you. My grandmother lived for games of chance, and the Scratch Offs provided many opportunities. Shug loved her vodka, and Phaedra brought bottles. Shug was easily won over.

On the other hand, my mother wasn't as easy to please, but she loved and admired Phaedra. She wanted whatever Phaedra had to rub off on me. Phaedra was independent, successful, and had money. She was a career woman, with a very bright future. I remembered the times when Phaedra would pick me up just to ride through the city in one of her expensive cars. We were big sh**! My feeling of self worth rose off the chains. Although we were two diametrically different people, our relationship strongly supported the theory that opposites attract. We talked to each other on the phone on a daily basis.

Phaedra was living the good life. The money and the cars, the entertainers and everything about her life, appeared to be so grand. It was the type of life I wanted, and I wouldn't stop until I possessed it myself. As our relationship continued to grow, I kept thinking that Phaedra was too good to hang around me and my crew. I mean, we were all from the streets. All of us were illegal, drug dealers, drug users, prostitutes, and hustlers. Some of Atlanta's finest, if I may say so myself. My title was hustler and I was a good one. This was a quality Phaedra may have seen in me.

I hustled whatever I could get my hands on. Everyone I knew, from family to friends, had some illegal kind of way to make fast money. Whenever they needed my assistance, I would provide my services for a small fee of course. My loyalty and good work ethics paid off. When someone wanted a job well done, I was that person they would call. Whether it was drugs, hot items, or my body, I did everything. From middle man, to the running man, and the front man, I played all the positions in the game.

Street life was my expertise until Phaedra started showing me a totally different lifestyle. We would attend some of the finest parties in the city together. She introduced me to fancy restaurants, and exquisite shopping boutiques.

December 31, 1999, Casper, a fellow hustler from the street who was close to me, was throwing a New Year's Eve bash in his penthouse. Casper was that real brother from another mother, as we say on the streets.

He always supported me, so I was planning to attend the event. Phaedra was my close friend, and made sure my clothes game was tight. She kept me up on the latest fashion and accessories. Phaedra hooked me up by sending me to the best boutiques in Atlanta, and I acquired the hottest in fashion. When New Years Eve finally rolled around, we were geared up to have a ball.

Phaedra and her brother attended the gala affair with me. We had such a fabulous time. There was a six-foot long cake, and countless tables of food. A live band played throughout the night, and revelers jammed to the latest tunes. Good music filled the air and I danced, feeling nothing but joy, joy, and more joy. It was a real celebration. We celebrated making it through the millennium alive, and the world had not been destroyed as everyone had predicted. I wasn't afraid anyway. Honestly, I felt that it would be better if we all died together. It wasn't like we could do anything about it if it had happened anyway.

Like a young doting sister, I loved and looked up to Phaedra Parks. There are times when I still do. She put me up on all kinds of game. She taught me to always look good, and act like I had money even if I didn't have a dime. She taught me to walk with my head held high, and never be ashamed of who I was or where I had come from. She always saw the greener side, and to her, nothing was the end. She felt everybody deserved a second chance. Her attitude was always positive. She had a can-do attitude and was always helping. She always preached that everything would be alright.

"It's where you are going, that should be your concern," she once advised me.

I remember that particular incident like it had happened yesterday. We were eating at Pappadeaux's Seafood Kitchen. It was one of her favorite place to dine. Her hair was pulled back in a bun. Her big eyes were dead-set on me. Phaedra spoke with so much conviction, she made me feel as if I was a child being reprimanded in a gentle way. It was just the way she spoke, and how she looked at me. This mild scolding had everything to do with her presentation, and I got it. I understood completely what she was saying, and I believed her! It was all about where I was going.

In a funny kind of way, Phaedra gave me my life back. A few months of hanging with her, and I had ceased being mean and so hateful. I also stopped dwelling on the past. Like sand in the hour glass, all the hurtful things I had been through, slipped away. Phaedra made me feel secure to be around her. I assumed that she was genuinely on my side. Meeting her actually gave me a chance to fix what was wrong with my life. It was an opportunity for me to grow as an individual. This was a chance to actually be somebody. That was all I really ever wanted—a chance.

I could never forget the year that Phaedra hosted her own Halloween birthday party. She was born at the end of October, and she organized a full scale, spare-no-expense, costume party—Phaedra style. It was very exquisite, and very tasteful. She was dressed as a cat. My cousin, Cookie, was a bunny rabbit, and I was a French maid. We had such a blast.

Drama showed up with another one of his girlfriends. That really

bothered me, but my girls were constantly in my ear, telling me to forget him. Especially Phaedra, Drama was her star client at that time, and she toured with him. She knew more about him and his lifestyle than I did.

Phaedra always told me that Drama was messing around with a bunch of other women. When she told me these things, she had no idea that Drama had been telling me that he had sex with her also. It seemed as if they were tossing me back and forth. So I disclosed to Drama that Phaedra had been telling me to leave him alone. This piece of news caused him to be very upset. He claimed that she was just mad because he wouldn't be with her only.

Thinking back, I found that their work relationship was quite un-usual. It seemed really odd for an attorney to travel on tour with clients. Once I told Drama how Phaedra hated on him, he swore up and down to me that he and Phaedra had a sexual relationship. I even had her call Drama on a three-way call, and remained silent on the line. He denied that they had ever had sex. Looking back, I realized that he knew that I was listening to the call. She had already prepped him on what to say, similar to the way she briefed all her clients. It was common protocol for Phaedra. She had mentioned this fact previously to me.

At the end of the day, all signs confirmed that Phaedra was a real freak. It was not a stretch to believe she had an intimate relationship with Drama behind my back. She even admitted it on national television, when she blurted out that her freak number was an eight or nine. Besides that, Drama had told me the same thing too many times, on too many different occasions.

Just about every conversation Phaedra and I had would result in her talking about sex. She would often elaborate about her performance of some type of sexual act. Phaedra threw herself at any man she felt she could benefit from, and that was just about any entertainer or athlete who showed interest. She even threw herself at my brother a couple of times. Lee always politely passed on her invites. He said, "She's not my kind of lady…"

I considered Phaedra a friend, so there were plenty of visits to her home. Some were for business, and plenty for pleasure. Sometimes I would visit her just so we could talk over a glass of wine. We talked about everything from men, clothes, sex, children, and the future.

She also shared her personal photo album with me. There was all kind of pictures of her dressed up as a dominatrix, bent over, and posing in different positions. I was shocked, but it didn't stop me from looking. Phaedra tripped me out, and I continued viewing the album, but I was mostly in disbelief.

I recalled the first time I visited her home on Oregon Trail in Marietta, Georgia. My cousin, Kate, tagged along with me on this particular visit. Now my cousin and I were known for cracking jokes, and talking bad about people. Just like any other buddies who were also family members, we shared a lot of laughs. Maybe it wasn't a good idea to invite my cousin, but it was already too late. Phaedra's home was nice, but was not all that fancy as I had thought it would be.

At the time, she was living in a three-bedroom, with two baths, and a two-car garage home. There was a small front yard, and the home was in a middle class neighborhood. Inside, maroon carpet was on the floor and when you walked in, the garage was located on the right. There was a big spacious living room on the left decorated in maroon and gold colors. The kitchen was located further down the hall. Her bedroom had a queen-size canopy bed and there was a master bathroom.

Her home was average, at best, but what really tripped us out was her bedroom. There was a pair of handcuffs attached to the headboard. Whips, and freaky-ass underwear were hanging everywhere. This was a den for S & M. Her tools were openly displayed as if she wanted people to know she was a freaky woman. In her bathroom, she had at least four thousand dollars worth of various makeup products scattered everywhere.

This scene was hilarious and ironic. Since she was a 'big-time', entertainment lawyer, we thought she would be somewhat conservative and modest, especially since she was the daughter of a preacher. Yeah right! Phaedra was into all kinds of S&M activities. Back in those days, everybody in Atlanta heard the rumors about her sleeping with over ninety percent of her clients. I didn't personally witness any of her sexual acts. Phaedra did talk about some things, sex was one of them, and she owned everything associated with a dominatrix lifestyle.

Phaedra loved to run her mouth about whatever she could find to talk about. So it came as no surprise when she gave me the inside scoop.

Like when Mystical was first arrested. Phaedra represented him as well. I knew a lot of details about him based on my conversations with Phaedra. So much for attorney-client confidentiality. One time, she talked really bad about Mystical's baby's mother. She told me about the time she first met the young woman at an area shopping mall. According to Phaedra, Mystical's baby's mother had some nerve being outside and wearing bedroom slippers. She kept insinuating how his baby's mother was soo ghetto despite all of the money generated from Mystical's musical success. At the very minimum, she thought the least he could do was buy the girl a nice pair of shoes.

I remember thinking, why was she so concerned about what the woman was wearing? Was she jealous? Of course, she was jealous because I'm quite sure she was screwing him too. It was obvious.

Mystical, if you read this book, you might want to ask Phaedra about your attorney-client privileges. I will not elaborate on too many details for the sake of Mystical, but I would like to say that Phaedra told me that Mystical was guilty, long before he was ever convicted. The hairdresser and those checks, right? Oh yeah… Yeah, I remember about you and your boys at the hotel.

Phaedra told me that Mystical was the dumbest motherf***** she had ever met in her life. She told me that his hairdresser, a woman that he had known for a long time, stole some checks out of his checkbook, and stole eighty-thousand dollars from him. Instead of calling the police, Mystical called the woman to the hotel under the pretension that he wanted his hair

braided. Then he and his entourage, raped the woman, beat her, and sodom-ized her! Phaedra Parks was absolutely livid.

Phaedra and I shared a lot with each other. I remember Phaedra call-ing me several times about a professional football player she was dating at the time. He dragged her butt through the ringer and she deserved it. She went through so much with this guy, and I could not understand why she was hav-ing these problems. I thought she was everything a man could want, and that any man would value and be honored to be in a relationship with a successful entertainment lawyer.

She was really hurt when she found out that her NFL ballplayer boy-friend had impregnated a stripper from Atlanta's infamous strip club, 'Magic City.' She went on and on about how the broad was nothing more than a strip-per, and that she was a lawyer. She just couldn't believe her boyfriend would stoop so low. Phaedra had spoken to me several times about this particular football player, and by her conversation she had high hopes for this relation-ship. Phaedra had mentioned to me previously that she assumed he was mess-ing around. I found out about him when she brought him up in a telephone conversation we were having one day. I considered myself to be a true friend.

"Look Phaedra you might be an intelligent, and successful super lawyer and all that, but that man has money too. Sometimes men like submis-sive and dependent women. They need to reinforce their power and domi-nance," I said to her, straight up.

Just because she had money and a name did not give her the right to handle a grown man any kind of way. Especially a man with his own money plus having his own name. It doesn't work like that.

Eventually, she began to realize that my input was invaluable when it came to love and relationships. I was amazed by the fact that my friend, an accomplished attorney, would call me for advice. I received a sense of validation from giving Phaedra advice because it made me feel needed. To top it off, I was usually right. Then it slowly dawned on me that because one had money, did not guarantee that one would have happiness.

From the NFL player, Phaedra moved on to dating a popular Atlanta radio personality. He was DJ Nabs of Atlanta's popular show, 'In the Lab with DJ Nabs'. She stalked this man. Please believe that! I promise you she did.

She would call him back to back, constantly trying to control him and his every move. She was a very demanding individual. I would ride with her by his house several times. She would just drive by to see if he was home. Then she would check out whose car was in his driveway, and if his lights were on, and peeped in to see if the TV in his room was playing. These actions would amount to stalking.

One night, it had to be during the summer of 2000, or around that time, I know it was warm outside, Phaedra and I rode over to his house. She had been calling him several times throughout that day and the evening. He hadn't responded or returned any of her calls. It was so obvious that he was avoiding her. So we drove by his house, only to find his car in the driveway.

She immediately jumped out of the car, and started peeping through his car window.

I felt like a fool, acting like a damn private investigator right along with her. But she was my friend, and I was down. Phaedra had good instincts because she was Phaedra Parks, the smart one. The big time lawyer noticed an umbrella in the back seat of his car. Of course, it was not just any old umbrella, she would later point out that it was decorative, with fancy carvings on the handle. No doubt, belonging to a woman.

I sat in the car and laughed like hell as she repeatedly kicked and banged on DJ Nabs' door. He refused to answer the door. It was at that moment when the realization hit me. Just because you are an attorney does not mean that everybody will kiss your ass. This was truly funny to me because I knew there had to be something else we could be doing. Besides, she didn't even like DJ Nabs! It was no secret that her relationship with him was for the benefit of her clients, which would in turn lead to profit for her business. DJ Nabs would be sure to keep her clients' songs in constant rotation. And that was cool, but right now she was just doing too much.

"Let's go get some money, Phae," I suggested with a smile written on my face. "You're tripping girl, and hard! It ain't that serious boo!"

She moved on, albeit with questionable choices. Even with all the various male conquests Phaedra had, I could not for the life of me understand where or how Apollo fit into her plans. Apollo was soon to become Phaedra's husband, but what was important here was that he was soon to be my future partner-in-crime!

Chapter Three
The Ties that Bind

"Faithful are the wounds of a friend; profuse are the kisses of an enemy..."
Proverbs 27:6 (NIV)

Our criminal activities began blossoming in 2000. It had been over a year of us feeling each other out. Phaedra was now comfortable enough to bring me into her illegal activities. She had gathered a lot of information about me—where I lived, where my mother and grandmother lived. She was familiar with all my hangout spots. I never perceived this as threatening because I was getting to know her better, as well. I knew where she lived, where she worked, and most, if not all, the people moving in her circle.

At first glance, Phaedra seemed completely concerned about my well-being. In retrospect, I can see how she brainwashed me. She told me that she wanted me to be her business partner because she liked the way I carried myself. Plus, the fact that I could hold an intelligent conversation would be a key in the success of Phaedra Parks Empire. She would tell me that I was the

only person capable of handling things in her absence. This business partnership was perfect. I was a hustler. I needed the money. I had three children, and all three were fatherless.

It seemed as if all my children were the results of a girl who was lost. I was trapped, looking for love in all the wrong places. Aleea, my first child was born in 1992. I was fifteen years old. Her father was sixteen years of age. He signed over all of his parental rights. We were just two kids having sex, and had no idea what being a parent meant.

Lekwaun was born in 1996 when I was nineteen years old. His father, a drug dealer, lived in and out of prison for most of his life. It was a quick romance and I thought it was real love, but turned out to be just lust.

Leontae was born in 1998. I was twenty-one years old. His father wanted to have unprotected sex but didn't want the child. I refused to have an abortion. He refused to be a part of the child's life. I was utterly confused and thought that if I had sex with a man, he would somehow care or love me in return. Being molested at five years old caused untold devastation. It took twenty-seven years for me to fully comprehend the difference between sex, lust, and love.

At that particular moment in time, all I wanted to know was what I had to do to get put on. I asked, "How do I benefit from our partnership, and how quickly can I get started?" Phaedra loved my 'go get them' attitude. Everybody did!

I was eager to get on board because I was struggling with financial hardship. There were limited options and I wanted my children to have the best of everything. I was a hustler and I didn't ask for handouts because I despised rejection. So no, I wasn't going to beg their fathers to be a part of my children's life. I wasn't going to hunt them down and fight them in court for twenty-five to the hundred dollars a week given in child support cases. That money was nothing! I would take care of them myself. You know the saying, "Mama's baby, daddy's maybe..."

It seemed like the perfect setup. I couldn't see how I would lose. I'd be making thousands of dollars working for my friend. She was one of the area's best attorneys who knew, and was the law as far as I was concerned. It was a no-brainer — the perfect opportunity. I was anxious to show and prove what an asset I could be to the team. In return, I would get my just rewards, of course.

Phaedra made a promise to me that I would make thousands of dollars. She told me that my kids would have a better life, and that I would never have to look back. The only thing I had to do was follow directions, and keep my mouth shut if ever I was questioned by the authorities. She knew about my past, and my troubled childhood.

She was aware that I was not afraid of anything. She also knew I had been to jail before. I knew what time it was, and was conscious of the inner workings of the system. Therefore Phaedra did not have to worry about me implicating her. I recognized when I should stay quiet. Being involved with the penal system in the past had left me thoroughly briefed.

When I was twelve years old, I was arrested for shoplifting. It occurred at the Main Place Mall in Buffalo, NY. The store was on the second level of the mall near the escalators. I took a white shirt, a navy blue and white polka dot skirt then left the store. I thought for sure that I had gotten away scot-free.

The skirt and the shirt were in my bag, and a hundred and fifty dollars was inside my pants pocket. Then as I rode the escalator down, I noticed the security guard at the bottom of the escalator. He was eagerly waiting, looking up at me. I turned around to run back up, and I spotted his partner. "Sh**!" I breathed under my breath. I was caught red-handed.

The total of the outfit was fifty-five dollars. My mother was so mad, I had the money, I just wanted to see if I could get away with the crime, but didn't. I got caught and they took me to the station and called my mother to pick me up. She couldn't understand why I would take the chance of shoplifting when I had money. I blew her wig back when I told her it was the thrill that I got out of doing it.

Before I met Phaedra I had been hustling and I have had several arrests for petty crimes. Including shoplifting, theft by receiving, giving false information, driving on suspended license, to plainly put it, I was a petty hustler and thief until I got on board with Phaedra.

She made a promise to me that if I ever got into any trouble, she would represent me. That was my security blanket. She told me that there was a secret society among lawyers and judges. Basically she made me believe, if

I ever got busted for anything, she would be able to get me off. This was due to her affiliations and influences. It was all I needed to hear. I was ready to go!

It started out very simple. Every morning, Phaedra and I had a meeting at either her home or her office she shared with another attorney at 1069 Spring Street in Atlanta, Georgia. Phaedra would provide computer printouts, fake identification cards, and fraudulent checks. The computer printouts contained brand names and the model numbers of specific electronic items. These included lap top computers, palm pilots, and DVD players, jewelry, home furnishings and televisions.

I always assumed she had money and couldn't quite understand why she needed such a large quantity of hot items. She never paid me for these types of jobs, but that was fine with me. My payment came in the form of additional checks she provided for my own use. There were no complaints coming from me. I had everything I wanted as well as a prepaid attorney on my side if things went bad. In this business venture, Phaedra provided her family, and friends with the latest in electronics for half the retail price.

I found out how superior Phaedra's operation was by the people she dealt with. When she called and told me to meet her at an office over on Northside Drive. I didn't know what to expect when I got there.

It was sunny out that day, but the wind had a strong force behind it. I arrived at around eleven o'clock that morning and hopped out of my favorite car, a 1982 Box Chevy Caprice Classic. It was all white with navy blue interior, wood grain steering wheel, super clean, everything original, beating the

block down with four twelve's in the trunk.

The heavy wind was blowing away everything that wasn't tied down. I was a six-foot tall, good-looking, young woman, and the wind was kicking so hard, I had to use my hand to hold my weave tracks in place. Phaedra waited on the other side of the parking lot holding the door open for me. The wind was threatening to close the door, and blow Phae's petite, almost five-seven frame back.

The inside of the building looked more like a warehouse than an office. The place was just a big empty space with one desk, three chairs, and dust. Phaedra introduced me as Dane, a nickname I had been given on the streets because of my height. It was short for Great Dane. I was introduced to the man sitting behind the desk, he was Alex. His face already looked familiar, but when she said his name it brought two and two together. Alex was the man! Alex Gidewon was the owner of Atlanta's hottest nightspot at the time, Club 112.

You didn't have to be from Atlanta to know about Alex or Club 112. It was a guarantee that you heard about him or read about him. Alex was a very well respected Atlanta businessman. I had seen him several times before when I visited the club. His tall slim build along with his caramel brown skin made him easy to remember. Every time I saw Alex, he was standing in front of the club making sure his business was operating smoothly, he never hid behind his desk.

He took a seat in a chair next to me, and listened as Phaedra gave me my instructions. My job for that day was to procure seven Dell laptop computers. She had given me the time frame. The merchandise was needed by eight that evening. I already knew that this would be a difficult task to accomplish. I could have easily gone to one store and purchased all seven of the computers, but that would've made things too hot. I didn't like drawing attention and preferred to remain all the way under the radar.

'Blend-in or bond-out' was my motto. By nine-thirty that evening, and five stores later, I had the order filled. Then I was on my way to see Phaedra to let her know that the mission was accomplished.

I was learning the ropes, and I had a damn good teacher. My mother always told me that I reminded her of a sponge because I was a quick-study. I had a photographic memory, and soaked up everything around me.

It amazed me that any person with any kind of government ID could write a check on a business account. I always thought it had to be that particular business owner. But to my surprise, I wrote checks well over ten-thousand dollars which were never verified or even questioned. Damn! Phaedra was one smart broad. I kept that bit of information under my hat because it was good to know for future references.

The game was set up like this, if I stole one of your business checks, I can make an exact duplicate of that said check. I can next go on a spree. Name or identification didn't have to match what was on the card. It could be any Jane or John Doe the check would still be approved as long as it was the same business account. If inquiries were made then I could easily report

that I was your associate in charge of whatever part of the business, secretary, or partner.

I treated my hustle just like a regular job. Rising at the same time everyday on go, I was just like the energizer bunny. In the end, my persistence paid off, and I was regimented. The job that I performed was considered to be business to business. I ran into and came across a lot of different people. One such person was a local rapper named, Slim. I fell in love with Slim the instant I saw him. Falling in love easily and immediately after meeting someone was a weakness I developed after being molested. It didn't take too much for me. I had developed a real need to be loved.

Of course I thought that Slim and I would be together forever. Everybody thought this way in the beginning of a relationship, and I was no exception. Slim was handsome. He was built just the way I liked my men, tall, dark and handsome. His skin was milk-chocolate brown and his body was a work of art. He had tattoos in all the right places. In addition, he was a hustler by nature. But it was his ambition and drive that really had me going. Ever since I can remember, I'd always been attracted to bad boys. Maybe because I was a bad girl, but I was ride or die type, without question. Slim was feeling me just as much as I was feeling him. From there, our romance continued to bloom.

January 2001, I became very ill. Throwing up, and the smell of certain types of foods made me really sick. I could barely stay awake and was always exhausted. Phaedra wanted me to pull a couple of stunts for her. The duties entailed going out, and writing some checks for electronic items. We had orders placed by her family, friends, and or associates to fill. I could hardly get out of bed and couldn't perform like I usually do.

I knew exactly what was causing my illness, but was in denial. Phaedra kept calling back to back. Until finally, I realized she just wasn't going to let me rest. I got up, dressed, and drove to her home. The moment she saw me, Phaedra could tell there was something wrong. I mentioned that I may be pregnant. She shook her head, grabbed her purse, and drove to the nearest drug store while I went to sleep in her bed. A trash can was strategically placed near the bed for any upheavals. I knew that I was pregnant again.

Phaedra returned with a pregnancy test kit and the test confirmed what I suspected. Phaedra immediately began pleading her case to the court. Of course, it wasn't a real court. I was being sarcastic, but she was pleading to me about why I didn't need more children.

She went on and on talking about how her criminal enterprise was in full force. The money was rolling in really good, and I was her MVP. She told me that if I had another baby it would slow down the entire business. Phaedra was right. I did not really want another child, and economically, I couldn't afford another child.

Phaedra made a telephone call, and after speaking for about ten minutes she hung up. I wondered what it was Phaedra had written down on her note pad. Then I found out that the person she had spoken to had given her some type of potion for me to drink. This concoction would cause me to have

a miscarriage. Phaedra and I headed to the grocery store where she purchased some kind of large red root. I had no idea what that sh** was. Honestly, I really didn't, but I trusted Phaedra. We immediately returned to Phaedra's home, and she boiled it along with some other ingredients. I drank the brew then waited for a reaction. We waited! We waited longer...! Still nothing happened! Damn! I began thinking.

Even though the concoction didn't work, Phaedra had convinced me that abortion was my only real option. When I told my baby's father about my plan to abort, he got on his hands and knees. Slim begged me to spare his child's life. Then he called my mother, and put her all up in my business.

By this time, my mother was a preacher. God had finally delivered her from low-down Curtis. She hadn't seen him for a year, and she was doing well living with me in Atlanta. There was absolutely no way she was going to stand by and let me abort her grandchild. Needless to say, I was stuck being pregnant and raising another child in addition to my three children. My family situation required steady financial gains. Making money quickly became the driving force behind my participation in all of the corruption.

March 2001, Phaedra introduced me to her current husband, Apollo Nida. He was clean-cut and very well spoken. About six feet two inches tall, intelligent and very handsome, Apollo put light skin dudes back on the map. He reminded me of a smooth criminal. Ironically, he even thought we were all crooks. For some reason, he came across as honest and sincere. Phaedra told Apollo that I was one of her closest friends, and her best worker. She explained that I had a proven track record, and it was time for my promotion.

This was the moment I had been waiting for and we met for hours that day. Finally, I was going to make the real money she promised me. No more running around to Best Buy, Staples, Office Depot, or Wal-Mart. I was tired of writing checks. Thus far, I had conducted our scam in every major department store in Atlanta. Therefore in order for me to continue to pull stunts involving writing bogus business checks to fill her daily orders, I would have to extend the boundaries of the operation. That would involve driving to the nearby cities and towns. I had hit the jackpot! I was pregnant. Simple trips seemed to take all day, and were becoming more tiresome. Phaedra called to inform me that she had something different for me to do. It was a good thing because I had told her on many occasions that I hated repetitive cycles. I needed something different.

By the way Phaedra was acting, I could tell that this gig was going to be the big one. I was ready for those thousands of dollars she promised I would make. Other than the one time I got caught, and was charged with forgery, everything Phaedra had told me to do seemed to have a smooth ending.

Even the one snafu or offense, I really couldn't blame Phaedra for that. She provided me with the checks, but I got banged up for personal purchases. She had nothing to do with that. I was out on bond awaiting trial. Phaedra assured me that I was only going to get a slap on the wrist. So again, I put my trust in her, and we kept rolling along.

July of 2001, Phaedra and Apollo drove me to Hartsfield Interna-

tional Airport. The previous day, I had given Phaedra a passport picture of myself that she instructed me to purchase from a CVS Pharmacy. I was told to go inside the airport, and purchase a round trip ticket from Atlanta to Washington, DC.

From the jump, I could tell that this particular operation would consist of some very slick, cunning and well-connected sh**! I did exactly as told and they waited for me outside the airport. My flight was due to leave the next morning. Everything was going according to plan. I left early that morning with a returning flight for later that day. I was given a folder filled with fake documents. I had in hand, bank statements, a utility bill, and a social security card with a fraudulent Georgia state driver's license.

The name associated with this particular operation was that of one, Tara Evans. The picture on the license was the same passport picture I had taken at the CVS Pharmacy two days earlier. Damn! I thought. The thrill of living life on the edge, playing with fire, and not getting burned gave me an adrenaline rush. They seemed to know their way around everything. I felt invincible.

My assignment involved flying to DC, and catching a cab from the airport to Baltimore, MD. Then I was supposed to go to the Department of Motor Vehicles, submit my documents, and obtain my State of Maryland driver's license.

I will never ever, ever forget that ride on the airplane that day. I was six months pregnant, overweight, and fighting with the father of my unborn child. To make matters worse, I did not know if I was going to make it back home. I just knew I was doing what I had to do.

There was a change of plans when I arrived in DC. What Phaedra and Apollo didn't know was that I had family there. I grew up in Buffalo, but I was born in Maryland. My mother had moved to Buffalo when I was six weeks old. DC was familiar territory. It just so happened that my uncle, Ernie, was in the hospital. Junior, my cousin, picked me up from the airport. He drove straight to the Walter Reade Memorial hospital where my uncle was on his deathbed.

Ernest Lee served our country from 1961 to 1997. He fought in the Vietnam War and was in Bagdad. He was retired, and had been a lieutenant colonel in the air force. Ernest Lee was my father's only brother. A family man and veteran, my uncle was in the hospital dying of brain cancer. Various family members told me that it would be a complete waste of my time for me to even visit him. They claimed he wouldn't recognize me, but I had to make this visit to see for myself anyway.

It was very painful for me to even imagine my uncle in that state, but I still wanted to see him. He had always been good to me, and never showed me anything but love. For that, I loved him. My uncle never treated me indifferently and I was sure he had heard all the bad stories about me.

Uncle Ernie had heard of the many schools which expelled me. He heard all about me being mischievous and disrespectful. Even when I got caught stealing, he heard about that too. My family members made sure they

told him of all the times I had run away from home, and the hell I dragged my father, his only brother, through. All those endless nights my father had spent searching for me my Uncle Ernie heard it all, but never once raised his voice to me. He never spoke anything foul about my life, and always offered me encouragement, no matter what kind of hell I put my parents through. He was never judgmental, and Uncle Ernie gave me his unconditional love. That was why the first thing I did when I landed in DC was to go visit with my sick uncle.

It was with some trepidation that my weak legs dragged me through the doors of the hospital. I quickly found his ward, and was soon standing next to his hospital bed, looking down at him. I glanced at the medical machinery all around him. Then reached out, and touched my Uncle Ernie's hand. I leaned closer to him.

"Uncle Ernie it's me, Angela. Your niece..." I whispered in his ear.

He knew exactly who I was. Instantly squeezing my hand, Uncle Ernie refused to let go. Tears began falling from his eyes. Deep feelings for him were welling up inside of me, threatening to explode. I knew I was on the verge of an emotional shipwreck, so I tried pulling my hand away. Uncle Ernie had a firm grip. It was getting emotionally out of control for me. After all, I was there to do a job and I did not have time to be sidetracked by my feelings for an ailing uncle.

With some hesitation, I began peeling his fingers away from my hand. Silently my tears rolled down my face while I severed our connection one finger at a time. I was thinking about his inevitable fate. Uncle Ernie was crying because he knew it was near the end for him. I had to seize control of my feelings, I broke free, and turned away. Walking out of his hospital room, I knew that it was the last time I would ever see my uncle alive.

Needless to say, the ride from the hospital to the Department of Motor Vehicles was not only stressful, but also unsettling. After all I was pregnant, my uncle was dying, and I was far away from home in another state doing something illegal. I had to put Uncle Ernie to the back of mind, and go handle business. My cousin, JR, pulled to a stop at the DMV. I sat adjusting my thoughts and makeup. It took a little while before I could completely detach myself and regain my composure before embarking on my mission.

Eventually I was able to confidently get out of the car. Knowing damn well that I had a handful of counterfeit government documents in my possession, I walked straight up to the counter without hesitation or fear. The DMV clerk viewed the documents, stamped them and told me to stand in line, and wait for my picture to be taken. I took my photo. Then the clerk gave me my new identity, and I proudly walked out of the DMV. I remember thinking how happy Phaedra would be when she knew I had scored once again.

I was happy to please Phaedra. In my mind, she had given me and my children a way out of poverty. Life was better now and I felt that I owed her for what she had done for me. I wanted her acceptance. I had always been an outcast. I was pleased to be accepted in her circle. I was relieved and glad that the mission was a success. I was also delighted that I had gotten away,

and contented about a job well done. With each success I received more clout and was advanced to the next level. I was rapidly climbing my career ladder. I didn't want to be viewed as a curmudgeon.

At around eight that same evening, I arrived back in the ATL. Apollo was waiting for me at the airport. Mission accomplished. It never dawned on me to even ask the purpose or what was to be the future use of the license. I trusted my partner, Phaedra, that much. There were no questions.

After a long, hard day, there was nothing more rewarding to me than to see the look on my mother's face when I returned home. At last, I was back in the comforts of my home. That whole day had just seemed so long and drawn out. My mother's whole life circled around my children, and me. She was unmarried and wasn't dating. My mother devoted her entire life completely to God. Joan Milling had been transformed into a very dedicated minister. My mother was a real preacher, and I was sure she would never give another woman a potion to abort an unborn child.

While she cared for my children, I provided financial support for my mother. At fifty-two years of age, she was a robust woman. But then one day, my mother got real sick. I took her to the hospital, and as I waited outside the hospital room, I overheard the doctor talking about my mother having breast cancer. The news of her condition was way too hard for me. Flipping out, I f**king lost it in that hospital.

Then came the many days and weeks filled with chemotherapy treatment. My mother's lovely hair began falling out. I hated seeing her sick. I couldn't handle seeing her on days when she could barely hold her head up. As a result, I sought to escape and spent most of my time on the streets. It felt safer out there. I focused on what made me feel good, and that outlet was getting money.

Having lost her business, and all of the benefits that came with it, my poor mother didn't even have health insurance for her treatment and medication. Even though I hated seeing my mother in pain, I felt powerless to really do anything to help her. There was nothing I could do to alleviate her hurting, and that made me angrier. I hated when things spun out of my control. I refused to see my mother suffer. Watching her going through her crisis made me feel like a victim. Those were images that I could never erase from my mind, and would vividly haunt me in my darkest hour.

I was a fighter and a survivor capable of giving super human efforts, but her illness proved to be the kryptonite. It weakened me, and out here on the streets, a fragile soldier will lose the battle every time. I needed my strength on a daily basis, and I walked into the lion's den seeking it.

My friends were but a few. I considered them all liabilities. During this time, some of my closest family members turned on me. They were jealous because I was managing to stay ahead. I constantly had to watch my

back. I scpoed not just for the police or the federal agents, but for my haters, and fake friends, the real enemies. My mother's sickness would only break me down. Therefore I was going to do whatever it took to make sure she had everything she needed.

After her chemotherapy treatments, the doctors said she was cured, but she never fully returned to her old self, not ever. My mother loved my children, and she always kept them with her. They were the loves of her life and her main concern. She always encouraged me to go to school or get a job, but she already knew that I was hardheaded, and wouldn't listen. She knew the only thing she could do for me was pray. Praying was what she did constantly, without ever ceasing.

One sunny morning at 8:47 a.m., Phaedra called me to her office. I had no idea what she had planned for me. I guess this was all part of her gimmick so that I would never be able to figure her out. When I walked through her office door, Phae had specific instructions for me.

"Take your Maryland drivers license along with this social security printout, and go to the Bank of America, downtown Branch on Peachtree Street and open a bank account," Phae said.

She also instructed me to deposit money and provide her with the account numbers. Phaedra Parks was about her business, and she did that very well. Later that morning, I left Phaedra's office on Spring Street. On leaving her office I opened the envelope, and counted the cash. Then I walked a couple blocks over to Peachtree Street.

Once the transaction at the bank was completed, I headed back to Phae's office, receipt in hand. This assignment was really simple. Of course, I was not afraid to open the bank account. It was not my name or social security number, but hell the bank teller was none the wiser. The driver's license I had in my possession was an official document. I knew that, so quite naturally I acted with confidence.

I never ceased to amaze Phae. Every time she sent me on a mission it was accomplished, and there were hardly any miscues. It wasn't like I was a dummy who had to call back just to find out what exactly it was I'm supposed to be doing smack-dab in the middle of the operation. Phae only had to instruct me once, and it was understood. My pregnancy was moving along fine, and I was getting closer to my delivery date. Phae was aware of this, so we had to move a little quicker on the operation. Unfortunately, we had to wait at least thirty days before there could be any major activity on the new account.

After the allotted time went by, Apollo gave me a check for $27,000 to deposit in the account. The check was from an insurance company and made out to my alias. I deposited the check, and Apollo told me that we had to wait five to seven business days for the check to clear. I was cool with that, but those five days were the longest days ever. I was tired of window-shopping, I was ready to go to the malls and buy everything I deserved.

The day Phaedra called my phone and told me the check had cleared was like sweet music to my ears. It seemed I had waited for her to call all my life. I knew how to handle my business. Straight up! I put on a navy blue

business suit and broke out my sophisticated wig. Then I met her at her office within forty-five minutes.

I had already told my baby's father, Slim, and my first cousin, Scott, exactly what was going on. I loved Slim, and told him about the business just to keep my end covered. My father always told me that there was no honor amongst thieves. People could be real shady when it was time to deal with a lot of money. I needed to make sure I had my end covered, just in case.

Scott was brought in because he was connected to the streets. Although, I trusted Phaedra, it was Apollo who I had a hard time trusting. I just wanted to make sure I got my chips at the end of the day. Those two were from the streets, and they did not trust Phaedra or Apollo. As a matter of fact, they didn't trust anyone.

Slim parked across the street from Phaedra's office, and waited. Then he followed our every move, oblivious to Phaedra and Apollo. Phae stayed in her office while Apollo and I went on the move. He drove to the first stop. It was the Bank of America located on Windy Hill in Marietta, Georgia. Apollo parked the car and, I walked inside the bank to make a withdrawal.

Now I'm going to keep it real, and let you all know that this time I was genuinely shaken. I was soo nervous, my knees were shaking, waiting for something to go wrong. It was going uneasily for me because I didn't want to go to jail, lawyered-up or not. Although I had an attorney, I didn't want to use her. I had been in the bank for about an hour. Apollo was calling on one line and Slim was calling on the other. I was trying not only to assure myself that everything was good, but I was also busy assuring them as well.

Then all of a sudden, the branch office manager asked to see me in her office. Now I was afraid. I was about seven months pregnant, and there was no way my fat-butt could outrun any of these folks. I was sh**ting bricks, thinking about what I was going to do next.

I knew that I had to maintain my composure. I kept it all the way cool walking closer to the manager's office. I was scoping out the layout of the branch and possible escape routes. The security guard was pretty much preoccupied. He didn't look at all concerned with my activities. Maybe the Branch Manager merely wanted to ask a few questions in private.

My heartbeat was getting louder with each step, but I cautiously followed the neatly dressed woman into her office. The moment we were inside, she politely gestured for me to have a seat. Then she closed the door. I was just about to scream bloody murder and act like I was about to go into labor, when she pulled out a brown paper bag. Whew! I thought. Thank you sweet Heavenly Father Jesus! I quickly and efficiently counted the money. It was exactly twenty-thousand dollars in cash. All big faces too!

It was the first time I had ever held that much money in my hands. I quickly placed the money inside my briefcase, thanked the bank manager, and quickly exited the bank. Apollo was waiting and I hopped into his BMW. Within seconds, we were out of there, putting distance between us and the bank. Apollo was smashing southbound on Interstate 75, doing about a hundred miles per hour.

This was one of the best feelings I had ever experienced in my life, getting away while carrying twenty-thousand dollars cash money. There was still seven-thousand dollars remaining in the account. I started wondering, what would become of it?

Apollo called Phae to inform her that we had scored a touchdown for the home team. I smiled when I overheard Phae bragging about me. He told Phae we had another stop, and after that we would link up with her. I was very excited about the money, don't get me wrong, but I kept thanking God that I had gotten away. I wasn't all that excited about going into another bank anytime soon. I mean, how many times can a person get away before that person is actually caught?

This was twenty-thousand dollars, and was a good number. I was cool with that, but Phaedra was greedy. She always had to have more. She wanted it all, and if I didn't get it all then I wouldn't be paid. The job had to be completed. I had Apollo and Phae on my team, and we were winning! I was ready to get it!

The next stop was the Bank of America on Piedmont Street. I walked inside the bank, again pushing any fear to the back of my mind. I walked back out of the bank with seven-thousand dollars cash. I gave Apollo the money to put with the other twenty-thousand dollars. He immediately called Phae and we met up at the Checker's restaurant downtown on 10th and Spring St. Then I called my baby's father and told him to meet me. He was already behind us anyway, but they didn't know that. Phaedra pulled up and hopped in the car with us. She gave me four grand. She and Apollo kept the rest of the money.

I eventually recognized that the four-thousand dollars was low pay for the high risk of my freedom. Being young and naïve, four-thousand dollars seemed like a lot of money to me at that particular time. Besides it was a little too late to start complaining about the money. I had agreed to the payment for my service beforehand.

We were at the office one day having one of our girl talks when I brought up Apollo's name. Phaedra seldom talked to me about Apollo. At the time, he was not her love interest and she told me often that he was nothing more than a worker and a plaything to her. When Phaedra told me that Apollo never satisfied her sexually, I knew then that their relationship was nothing more than a game for her. I didn't ask, she just decided one day, to blurt out that Apollo had only one testicle.

"What the hell? Phae girl, you crazy as hell!" I laughed at the time.

After working with Apollo, he and I became cool. He was my partner. While Apollo and I ran the streets, Phaedra was able to sit hidden away behind her desk. Apollo was never disrespectful, and was always about his business. I respected that!

I was being a sh**-starter. So I told Apollo about the conversation me and Phae had about him. Phaedra had not mentioned to me that she was

serious about him or that she had any intentions on being with him. I felt like she didn't give a damn, so I didn't either. I also wanted him to know that I knew his business. I wanted to see his reaction, it may not have been right, but it was really hilarious at the time

I thought he was going to be cool, calm, and collective about it. Turned out, he wasn't. He called Phae right there on the spot and, oh Lord, did it go down behind her disclosure about his private parts. That was very personal for him. I could tell by the way he handled the situation that it had hurt him deeply. He explained that it was caused from a motorcycle accident. Wow, he really did have one testicle. Phae laughed like hell about it. She even called me on a three-way call a day later to let me hear his ranting and raving.

She wanted to go out of her way to show me that she could care less about his feelings, and she didn't give a damn about me telling him what she said. It was a joke to her. She laughed, I laughed and we both really laughed after hearing how he snapped on Phaedra. He was crying like a baby.

Apollo was absolutely livid. That was so crazy. I knew then never to tell him anything. He had gotten too emotional. I figured that he had to be raised by women. Most of the males I knew who were raised by women tended to be very emotional.

Children learn what they see. If every time something goes wrong

and the reaction they experience were tears and screaming, then they tended to cry and scream. If they see someone standing strong and addressing what actually went wrong without emotional outburst then they would address problems that way. If a child was born in a home where only English was spoken, that child would speak only English.

With the money I made from the bank job, I bought a car from my brother. Got everything my children needed, gave my mom some money, and purchased some things for the new baby. Before I knew it, that money was gone just as quickly as I had gotten it.

Chapter Four
Whispers and Warnings

"Then whosoever hear the sound of the trumpet,
and take not WARNING; if the sword come, and take him
away, his blood shall be upon his own head."

Ezekiel 33:4 (NIV)

In October of 2001, I gave birth to my son, Jayvien. Phae was crazy about my baby. My baby's daddy and I were on the verge of breaking up. Obviously, I was too much for him and quite frankly, this man could not handle me. I will admit that I was being your typical ghetto female. I was plugged in, I was affiliated, and I didn't need him. As far as I was concerned, he needed me. He would do disrespectful things like have females call my house for him, and that did it. I was not one to tolerate disrespect, so I left him and started messing around with Drama again.

Two months later, my trial date for the forgery charges had come and gone. I had several ID's so it wasn't my desire to answer the charges or

to serve any time. In my little mind, I was balling hard, and never even went to court. At this point, I became a fugitive from justice. The state of Georgia was now looking for my dumbass. However, I wasn't worried one bit by this. Because of my connections, I felt like I was a made-woman. Slim was very aware of what I was doing, and who I was running with. I was a product of Phaedra Parks, and had several identities. I didn't believe I would ever be caught. Like a true mafia outfit, we were operating above the law, and I was in an elite network of workers for Phaedra Parks. The only way they would catch me was if someone snitched.

It was the beginning of a cool summer day. The early morning dew had just set, and a steady breeze seeped through my upper bedroom window. Drama and I were lying in bed. I had just come back from the store. I was fully clothed, but he was butt naked. My cellphone started ringing back to back. It was Jayvien's dad, another local rapper known as Decatur Slim. Needless to say, there was already animosity. Drama was a top guy in the music business while other rappers were still trying to get noticed by the industry. The last thing I wanted was a confrontation between the two of them. Decatur Slim was fully aware of my previous dealings with Drama and everybody in Atlanta knew that Drama drove a white Mercedes-Benz truck. I didn't have a garage so when Drama visited he would always park his truck right in front of my door.

BAM! BAM! BAM! There was a loud banging on my door. I started to the door, wondering aloud.

"What the hell? Who is banging on my door like that?" peeking out the peephole. "Oh Lord, it was my baby-daddy! Damn! Okay... Think!" I said to myself. Then quickly, I tried to surmise the situation. I couldn't call the police because I was as hot as a firecracker. I could just ignore the banging on my door. I knew damn well, that I had told this man we were over. Why in the world would he be at my door acting like a damn fool?

By this time, Drama was all in my ear, asking me what was going on. So I told him everything was good. Slim would leave in a minute, and the banging would cease. Drama was already agitated and was now screaming in my ear.

"Do you know who I am? Why do you have me in this predicament?"

A minute later, my baby-daddy was coming up the stairs. This man had climbed straight through my kitchen window. All I could think was I'll just be damned! There wasn't enough time to hide. I knew I was going to have to fight this crazy man. He saw Drama lying in my bed, and went berserk.

Please do not get this twisted. I wasn't some small, petite, frail type. I wore size twelve shoes and was six feet tall, looking damn good too. Okay? So please don't get me wrong, I grew up with an older brother, a bunch of boy cousins, and fear was something that never gripped me.

My baby-daddy knew full well that I could handle myself, and so did Drama. I mean Slim and I were thumping. Blow for blow, we went tumbling down the stairs. My weave was ripped out and everything was out. This

was all out war. He was fighting because his feelings were hurt and I was fighting back because I had no other choice.

While we were scuffling Drama managed to walk out unnoticed. That sorry-ass-dude didn't even try to break up the fight. He just broke out! What the fu**! My neighbor heard the commotion and the police were summoned. When the police arrived, my crazy baby-daddy gave them my real name. Of course, when the police ran the requisite background check on me, my outstanding warrant popped up. Then they promptly hauled my dumbass off to jail. I served four months in Washington State prison. My light sentence was like a slap on the wrist to me.

I had money put up and Phaedra kept money on my books. She readily accepted all my phone calls. I also knew that as soon as I touched down, there would be a job waiting for me. With my money up, I called home every single day and made sure money stayed on my books. The trip to prison was more like a vacation to me.

When I touched down, I made one phone call to my big dog, Phae. She was real glad to hear that I had been released. It was already understood that I would meet with her once I had spent some time with my mother and children. I was surprised to see how much my kids had grown in that short time span. My mother told the children I was away at college. She told that lie truly out of motherly love. She never talked badly about me around my children, and just like me, she demanded respect.

Decatur Slim, my baby-daddy, and I were done for good. There was no way I could allow myself to be with anyone who would think of selling me into slavery. Oh hell no! Forget that! Baby or not—it was a wrap for his ass! There was no compromising. I was gone with the wind. Everything about me was illegal, and that made him a liability.

Two weeks later, Phaedra and I were back to business. Phaedra informed me that Apollo would be out of the picture for a while. He had gotten knocked on another case in Newton County while I was temporarily away serving my bid. We agreed to meet at her office later that day. She wanted me to meet someone. This person would be Apollo's replacement.

"Cool," I said.

I couldn't wait. By any means necessary, I knew that money was a necessity. Phaedra's schemes were clever and elaborate. She never ceased to astound each and every time she approached me with an assignment. On numerous occasions, I often found myself excited about learning her tricks of the trade.

I would like you to think about it for a minute. Please, relax and breathe. Now analyze the state of affairs for a moment. Phaedra was this crooked attorney who knew how to commit crimes against the federal government. She also knew how to get away with it. Phaedra Parks studied the law extensively, and learned how to manipulate the cracks in the system.

Our meeting was scheduled for three in the afternoon at Phae's office. I didn't think twice about the person she wanted me to meet. If there was one thing I knew about Phae, it was that she was always a business woman first, and she kept her business wrapped tight. She was a consummate master of her trade. For that reason alone, I never felt a need to question her tactics.

She introduced me to a five-foot-ten-inch, pale complexioned man known as E. The most intriguing thing about him was his hazel eyes. They were the same color as mine. Actually they were just like my father's. I took this to be the number one indicator that this dude was a slick one. So was I as well as my father. I didn't hate on him, especially if Phae brought him onboard.

By the time I left that meeting, whew boy, my mind was racing. Phaedra was witty. Her ideas, her brain, and the way she orchestrated things, so clever. It did not cross my mind that I would or could even get caught. It all just seemed so simple back then. We were above the law. Hell as far as I was concerned, we were the law. Thanks to you know who.

Phaedra was the answer to everything. The only thing I really needed to know was how to act. All my life I always believed that acting was part of my God-given talent. Along with hustling, acting came natural. I began thinking of myself as this smooth criminal. I had gotten accustomed to the quick money by now, and quite naturally I never turned down any jobs, no matter how high the risk. The next mission would be one of the biggest jobs ever assigned to me by Phae. The assignment was well thought out, strategized, and planned. The factor of time was very important in the execution of this mission. Combine this with patience, and it became very demanding. These types of jobs have to crawl before they mature and start walking. Then low and behold, before you even know it, they were off and running.

The first part of my assignment involved scoping out potential vehicles at luxury car dealerships. Each day I simply drove around Atlanta, and the surrounding cities looking for potential prey. Every car lot I visited had several luxury cars. I spotted all of the latest models of Porsche, Mercedes Benz, Hummers, Corvettes, and Cadillac.

After selected luxury dealerships were identified, I would then walk around the lots with pen and pad. I casually, but discreetly recorded the VIN numbers, makes, and models of not only the latest, but the hottest whips to hit the city.

Once I had the information recorded, I reported it back to E. We rarely discussed business on the phone. So E and I met daily, and swapped information, and fake documents. It seemed like we never stopped. I provided the VIN numbers, and he gave me the fake identification cards, and fraudulent registration cards matching the vehicles I had previously recorded. At this point, I was handling all of the day-to-day operations.

Phae never had to worry about the illegal side of the operation. She was a very busy woman, and spent all of her time managing her thriving law practice. Honestly, everything with me was infallible. Phae knew as long as I was on the assignment, she would get her money, and remained focused on

the affairs of her clients.

With the state issued ID, and proof of ownership, I would be able to visit any other luxury car dealership, provide them with the necessary documents as well as a fee, one hundred and eighty dollars at that time. Then just like that, they would cut a computerized key to the vehicle.

The second part of the scheme involved a late night visit when the dealership closed down. We would return to the dealership and drive away in brand new vehicles, with no disturbances. Even if we did run into a problem such as getting pulled over by the cops, we had all the right paperwork in our possession. The right key and a bill of sale that could be verified by the police. They would never suspect anything because the vehicle hadn't been reported stolen.

The cars were then sent to a chop shop. The VIN numbers were filed down, and replaced with new ones. Once replaced, I was provided with fraudulent certificates of vehicle titles from the state of Ohio. It seemed like I was going back and forth to the Department of Motor Vehicles in Hapeville, Georgia, on a daily basis. The Ohio titles had to be swapped out for Georgia. No ifs, ands or buts about it, which was an important step of the scam.

There were other areas of the business which required my utmost attention. This was a major operation, and I could only be in one place at a time. Phae insisted that I enlisted the help of my cousin, Sheree. She too was a go-getter, and Sheree was about her business as well. Anything having to do with making money, she was with it, and so was I.

Sheree would now assume the position off title-swapper. Her job was to visit the Department of Motor vehicles at least twice a week. Relieving me of that duty, she was giving me time to actually enjoy my private life. As all young women do, I found myself right back in love again. This time, I thought for sure it would be different and actually last.

He was older, more mature, and intelligent. Shaheed was considered a boss on the streets of Atlanta. He had money, power, and was well respected wherever he went. This gave me a feeling of superiority. I was caught up in the excitement of being Shaheed's girl. There were great rewards and major benefits.

The biggest incentive of being in this relationship was that anyone who knew him, and was aware of my ties with him, gave me the highest respect possible. In fact, if I even looked as if I had a problem, all I had to do was mention his name, and my problem went away instantly. Love was in the air and my aura of invincibility had suddenly grown way beyond my wildest imagination.

He was a Muslim brother, and Shah was ruggedly handsome as he was tough. I had never been involved with a Muslim before. To say the least, I was intrigued by his dedication to his family, and religion. Watching him going through his religious ritual of praying five times a day, no matter what he was doing or where he was, was itself an attractive thing.

I had heard the rumors floating around the city about Shaheed, but didn't pay them any mind. There were claims of him being a hit man, a murderer, and the devil. The list would go on and on. He never gave me any

indication that he was anything like what people were talking about. But he did tell me about the violence that occurred when he was still a child.

Shaheed was only six years old when his mother was brutally murdered. She was seven months pregnant and was stabbed twenty-seven times. Her throat was slit, and even though he was terrified, Shaheed was forced to watch this heinous crime. Then the murdering son of a bi**h threw the young, innocent Shaheed into a closet. Scared to death, Shaheed waited in the dark closet until he was discovered two days later.

After hearing his painful story, and all the rumors about him, I knew it was dangerous to be involved with Shaheed. But I also knew, just like me, Shaheed was a victimized child. For that reason alone, I saw a light shining in him when other people only saw darkness. He was a product of his environment, and a victim of his own circumstances. That did not make his actions right and I was in no way condoning the decisions he made, but I understood his pain.

In the three months or so that I had known him, Shaheed was always kind to me, and had never done me wrong. Something inside wouldn't allow me to accept that the man I had fallen in love with could be a cold-blooded murderer. Even Phaedra had heard the stories about him. Anyone we came across who knew anything about Shaheed had the same thing to say.

My take on Shaheed was much different. He had a job and a religiously, healthy routine for living. He was an excellent father and provider. Shaheed was a wonderfully gifted and passionate lover. There was nothing about him indicating he was even capable of committing the kind of monstrous acts I had heard about on the streets. He appeared as an angel of light.

He would stop by Phaedra's office whenever I was there. He was my protector and knew about the business between me, Phaedra, and Everett. Shaheed had no problem letting them know that he was there to make sure all the business ventures went smoothly. Everett aka E was affiliated with the west side of Atlanta. He was well aware of Shaheed's reputation on the streets, and now approached me with extreme caution. E did not want any problems.

Shaheed liked kicking it with me, and Phaedra. Phae was crazy, and would run her mouth about anything. I remember one day we were sitting in her office and somehow we got on the topic of oral sex. I was very, very uncomfortable, but it was Phae, Shah, and me. So I thought not too much of the conversation. Phae decided to share the intimate details on the proper way to perform oral sex. Suddenly she began demonstrating with her lips, mouth, tongue, and hands.

I glanced at Shaheed. He was sitting directly across from me and looked like a little kid in a candy store. Wait, a candy store would be an understatement. Let's say, Willy Wonka's factory. He was wearing this huge grin, stretching from ear to ear on his face. Then out of nowhere, Shaheed said, "Aye! So you mean to tell me that you're the one who taught her that? Well, let me be the first to thank you! Really!" Then he continued shouting, "Certified head-doctor." This was now Phaedra's official street name. Didn't I tell you from the beginning that ol' girl was a freak?

In August 2003, I found out I was pregnant again. This time Phaedra had nothing to say. I guess she just figured I was going to be pregnant every year anyway. I believe that as long as she got paid her money, she didn't really care one way or another. It was business as usual. Everything was moving right according to the plan, until a few months later. Sheree was held and questioned at the Department of Motor Vehicles Title office in Hapeville, GA.

Peter McFarland, an auto-theft detective, happened to be on duty that particular day when Sheree followed her usual routine. At this point, we were being watched and investigated for months without our knowledge. Detective McFarland was waiting on either of us to walk through the door of the Hapeville office. When Sheree arrived, she was questioned, and detained. Eventually she was released. Sheree called me as soon as she could.

Sheree claimed that the authorities had drilled her over and over again, asking her where she had gotten the titles. She reportedly told them that she met a woman who gave her a power of attorney, and paid her to transfer the titles. Sheree told me that they showed her a video of me, and wanted to know my identity. She acted ignorant, and swore up and down she didn't know me personally. The whole operation was now in jeopardy. Hell, my freedom was now at risk! I immediately called Phaedra and Everett. We scheduled an emergency meeting.

An hour later, Shaheed and I arrived at Phaedra's office. Nobody seemed to be in panic mode but me. We were so close to the big score! Everything had already been setup and put in place. The vehicles were clean and ready to go. Phaedra firmly insisted we move forward, and proceed as planned with the operation. It was decided that Everett, my cousin, and me would head for Chattanooga, Tennessee, the very next morning with three of the luxury vehicles.

That whole evening, nothing sat well with me at all. Sleep came slowly, and I restlessly stayed awake most of the night. Staring at the ceiling, I had a flurry of thoughts going in my head. I had always believed everything Phaedra had told me. So far things were so good, and I didn't have anything bad to say about her. I couldn't remember a time she had told me anything wrong. If Phaedra told me it would work then it worked!

Chapter Five
Road to Redemption

"Now when these things begin to take place, straighten up and raise your heads, because your redemption is drawing near."

Luke 21:28 (NIV)

I awoke earlier than usual. I prayed just as I always do every morning, hoping that God would be with me as He always was. Daylight seemed like it came a lot quicker. Maybe it was the fact that I was pregnant and didn't sleep well. Whatever it was, a sick feeling surged through my gut as I got out of bed. By the time I was getting dressed, my mother was already up, and she was in the kitchen cooking breakfast.

She had been up most of the night because that was when she liked to pray. She would pray when it was silent or when my children were asleep. She said, "In the dead of the night, was when I can really focus solely on praying to our Heavenly Father."

That morning Shaheed came by earlier than usual. Before you knew

it, we were arguing about him not being there with me the previous night. Despite our minor dispute, he had brought me my usual morning cravings, oranges and hot chocolate. Being that I was seven months pregnant at the time, Shaheed didn't allow me to even bend over to strap on my shoes. He knelt down, and fastened my shoes. Shaheed was busy with the task at hand when in a smooth, calm voice I said, "Shaheed, what if I don't come back?"

He looked up at me and said, "You're coming back! Don't think like that kiddo! Let's go handle this business."

I kissed my babies goodbye. Then I paused before walking out the door. I stared longingly at my mother, I didn't imagine that this would be the last time that I would ever see her. Sheree had gotten nabbed and I was worried. But we were above the law, getting caught crossed my mind, but I refused to believe it could happen. Sh** was getting hot, but I wouldn't let my fear stop me.

When I left home that beautiful, sunny morning in the middle of March, I didn't leave with the intentions of never returning. I left out my house in the hunt to put food on the table. Just as the lioness would leave her cubs in search of food, with plans to return, and feed her family, so was my plan. But sometimes things don't always go the way we planned. Do they?

Even though I was tired, I knew we were heading down to Chattanooga, TN. My job was to drive one of our luxury vehicles to the dealership. Then hand them my title, my driver's license, and my proof of registration when I got there. I was to explain to them that I wanted to trade my expensive car for a vehicle that was a little less flashy. In return, they would give me a car of lesser value, and also cut a check for the difference. The amount was usually over twenty thousand dollars. That was the plan. It seemed easy enough.

I was driving up Interstate 285 toward 75 N to meet Everett, and my cousin, my cellphone rang several times. It was my mother calling.

"Forget this one. Please come back," she pleaded. "Come back for your children's sake…"

My mother was begging for me to turn around and come back home. I had to do what I had to do. My mother knew I wouldn't listen to her. I never did in the past.

"I'll be back as soon as this over," I assured her, hanging up quickly.

She called a couple more times, but after I ignored her calls, she eventually stopped calling. We were too close for me to throw in the towel. All I had was my word and I had given it. What would Phaedra think if I decided to back out at the last minute? She'd probably never forgive me. My name could possibly be slandered. The truth was that the authorities were already looking for me. If I screwed up with her, I'd be assed-out for sure! So f**k it! I thought driving.

We met up at the rendezvous, and with Everett in lead position we drove behind each other all the way to Tennessee. I had no idea where we were, how we got there or how to get back to Atlanta. Then Everett pulled into a Waffle House across from the first car dealership. We followed right behind him. He parked his car, and jumped into the truck with me. He handed me a walkie-talkie along with all of my fake documents. I left Everett and

my cousin at the Waffle House. I went to the car dealership, scoped out my surroundings, and went inside to make the transaction.

After assessing the vehicles on the car lot I finally made a decision on which vehicle I would purchase as part of the scam. I selected a 1992 Nissan Stanza in return for a 2003 Cadillac Escalade. I even took the car on a test drive. Upon my return, while waiting on the paperwork to be drawn up, the car salesman asked for the city, and state I was born in.

"What?" I shot back while quizzically looking at him.

This was a question I wasn't prepared to answer. The good attorney, Phaedra Parks or Everett hadn't prepped me for this question. I just blurted out the first thing that came to mind.

"Detroit, Michigan." I said, after a few nail-biting seconds.

I had no idea that the first three digits of your social security number identified the state you were born in. He wrote down my answer and walked off. I should have focused more on the way he walked out of the office. I quickly went to the bathroom and hurriedly called Everett. I was asking him why that question was relevant, and why was it taking so long.

Everett claimed that everything was alright. He told me I was doing fine, and to just go back inside and wait on the paperwork. I did as I was told. But something just didn't feel right. About ten minutes later, he was on the walkie-talkie shouting, "12, 12, 12..." This was our code for the police.

Glancing around in a frenzied panic, I could immediately feel cold sweat dripping down my white silk top. My breath was coming hard and heavy. I felt my head frantically moving side to side then back and forth like it was on a swivel. Oh my God! I was pregnant, and what was I going to do? I started running around in circles, pacing back and forth, searching for an avenue of escape. All I could think about were my children and how I had to make it back home. Suddenly, I took off running! I ran straight out the back door of the office. Running through the lot, I could see Everett on the ramp already making a run for the highway. I had the walkie-talkie to my mouth yelling.

"E! Don't leave me! I can make it! Stop! E!" I screamed into the walkie-talkie.

I was pregnant, sprinting behind the truck, and begging him. Everett never glanced back. The truck just kept on going, and didn't look as if it was going to stop. Breathing hard, I kept running for dear life! It was me and my precious baby. They weren't catching us, I kept thinking with every step.

The police, however, finally caught up with me. An officer who was paid to uphold the law, slammed me on the asphalt while kneeing me in my back.

"I'm pregnant! I'm pregnant!" I shouted repeatedly.

The officer didn't seem like he cared, one way or the other. He was angry that I had tried to outrun him. It wasn't until another officer arrived that they realized I was in fact pregnant, and that I was in severe pain. Bruises were all over my body when they transported me to Skyridge Medical Center, a local hospital.

Tears had not set in yet. I was still trying to figure out how I was going to get out of this situation. That was when reality and the humiliation

of my dire situation began to quickly set in. I knew I was f**ked. Shackled to the hospital bed, I was in total disbelief. I was in a state of shock while awaiting the arrival of the auto theft detectives.

I closed my eyes tightly, and saw my whole life flashing in front of me. This was it, I surmised. How was Phaedra going to work her magic in Tennessee? Did she even have a license to practice in this state? What about my mother and my children? My mind was traveling a hundred miles an hour, but there seemed to be no quick resolution. Then abruptly, my thoughts crashed. My life of crime had come to a screeching halt.

Mentally, I was still searching for an escape hatch. There was a phone on the side of my bed, and an officer posted outside my door. He was standing there like I was an assassin or serial killer. My handcuffs were loose, and I had already slipped them off. Now I just needed to figure out how to get out of the hospital. When I looked to my left, the window was open, and I could see that I was on the ground level. Perfect opportunity!

Then Shaheed ran across my mind. I called and told him that I had been arrested. He was very upset. This wasn't part of the plan he reminded me. I could tell by his voice that he felt completely powerless. I told him I could break free. The only thing I needed was for someone to be outside the hospital waiting for me. Shaheed immediately called E and advised him that it would be in his best interest not to return to Georgia without me. E came back to the hospital. I guess he was wandering through the halls trying to find me. He knew the last thing he needed was a problem with Shaheed.

Everett was arrested in the hallway of the hospital. When the auto theft detectives arrested him, they came straight to my room. Apparently, Everett had been to Tennessee several times before with the same scheme. So the auto detectives already knew who he was, and were patiently awaiting his return. That's when I started wondering, where the hell was Phaedra Parks?

Things got a little crazy for me at this point. I just couldn't, for the life of me, understand why E would bring us back to a place they had already burned out. I mean if you just robbed a bank last month, and got away. Why in the world would you want to return to the scene of the crime, trying to rob the same bank again? The auto theft detectives began drilling me with questions.

"Who are you?" This big, heavyset, white guy with wide nostrils shouted. "How did you get involved with these people?" he asked with no regards for sympathy. "Do you know how much trouble you are in?" "How many children do you have?" "Where are you from?"

Agitated, I stared past the detectives, refusing to answer any of their questions. If they had me, then they were going to have to show me they had me. Even though I had been caught red-handed, with my hand all the way down in the cookie jar, I refused to help them indict me.

The questioning went on and on. Their frustration with me was getting obvious. I knew not to say one single word. I just sat there and kept staring at the wall. They told me that I was only hurting myself. Then they walked out of the room. Three days later, I was transferred from the hospital to Hamilton County Jail in downtown Chattanooga, Tennessee.

My incarceration didn't come with any kind of surprises. I had already suffered over thirty arrests and or run-ins with the law. So I knew the drill, and I knew how things worked.

I just wanted to get booked, so I could bail out. I did the only thing I could do to help myself which was call my mother. My mother was already ten steps ahead of me. She already knew how much my bond was and was prepared to pay it. She had already talked with Phaedra who informed us to just be cool and not speak to anyone. But there was a problem. Although I did in fact have a bond, I also had a hold in Clayton County, Georgia for the fraudulent car titles.

If my mother paid my bond, I would be released but they would release me to the Clayton County, Georgia authorities. My charges in Hamilton County, Tennessee were all associated with the false identity. These charges were serious, just not as serious as the charges I faced back home in Georgia. Another problem my mother would probably encounter in trying to pay my bond was the fact they could argue that I was going to be a flight risk since I lived in another state. I was in a world of trouble and I knew it. I told my mother to hold onto her money because I knew she was going to need it.

I decided to sit, and wait for Clayton County.

Knowing that I was going to be there for a while, I worked toward making myself as comfortable as possible. I was getting acclimated to my surroundings when a few days later, my name was called over the loud speaker. I thought it may have been my mother coming to see me. It wasn't. The Georgia Bureau of Investigations (GBI) paid me a visit. They handcuffed me, placed me in the back of their vehicle, and transported me to another location.

I was riding in the back of their vehicle, and couldn't figure out for the life of me why they had me. What did they want from me? I had never had any dealings with the GBI and the FBI. My stomach was doing flips, and my mind was racing as I kept wondering what this latest development was about. Lord, Lord, what have I gotten myself into now?

Chapter Six

A Bottomless Pit with No Way Out

"No temptation has seized you except what is common to man. And God is faithful; he will not let you be tempted beyond what you can bear. But when you are tempted, he will also provide a way out so that you can stand up under it."

1 Corinthians 10:13 (NIV)

I was placed in a small room with a long table at the end. My handcuffs were removed then I was offered coffee and cigarettes. Coffee...? Yes, but cigarettes were definitely not my thing. I hated the way they tasted, the way they smelled, and the way they made you feel.

Special investigators had never questioned me before so this was very scary for me. I remember watching how these interrogations went on television cops and robbers movies. Mentally preparing myself for the whole

good cop, bad cop scenario, I would be ready.

Through it all, I believed I remained as strong as I could. What was done was done. It made no sense crying over spilled milk. So let us do what we have to do, and move on from this. These thoughts were flowing through my mind while I waited. I had resolved to push through this barrier. It was working just fine until the bad cop opened his mouth.

"Ms. Stanton, let's cut straight through the BS! Tell us all about Leonard!"

"Leonard? Who the hell is Leonard?" I asked, staring wide eyed at him.

The detective was short and stocky. He looked just like one of the kids I had picked on in school. Except he was grown up, and was about to pay me back for every name that I had ever called him. His receding hairline, and overgrown beer belly made me look at him with a more serious attitude. He was the type of person that needed just a little bit of authority. And I didn't think he had been around too many black people in his life. In my mind I placed myself back at the chessboard with my dad, remembering every move he had ever taught me, before I started speaking again.

"I don't know anybody named Leonard!" I yelled.

The detective looked at me in disgust as if I had just murdered his only child right before his eyes. Without hesitation, he slung a manila file folder as thick as the yellow pages with Shaheed's picture on the front of it. I watched it as it slid from his end of the table all the way across the table, and down toward my end of the table. It abruptly stopped in front of me.

Befuddled, I didn't know what to think. Maybe they had been watching us, and had pictures and paperwork from monitoring our every move. I didn't know what the hell was going on until I looked at the picture on the front of the folder. My mind was whirling in the wind of possibilities when glanced at the detective. With resentment in his eyes, he stared at me and calmly said, "Ms. Stanton, if you want to ever see that baby you're carrying, you will tell us everything that we want to know. We don't take threats taken out on federal agents lightly."

I was shaken and really couldn't figure out what was going on. Still in shock from learning that Everett and Phaedra had sent me back to the same car lot they had just burned, I felt like this was all part of a set up. They had been driven by greed. This situation with Shaheed had me scared and confused. I was still trying to figure out how the detectives knew about Shaheed. The detectives seemed to know more about me, and my life than I did. I was scared to death, and felt very ignorant. Everybody seemingly knew what was going on, except me. I realized that I was in way over my head.

My mind kept drawing blanks. I was at a total loss for words. Reality had me so shook that for a minute everything seemed blurred. Finally, I slowly came back around, but was still stuck trying to comprehend what exactly the detective was saying. It did sound like he had just said Shaheed threatened a federal agent.

O-o-okay! If he did, what did that have to do with me? I was being held for auto theft, and giving false information. Even more surprisingly, how did they link me to Shaheed? Someone was talking, and it wasn't me.

Shaheed had nothing to do with why I was in Tennessee. Who was talking to these detectives or had they been just watching us? This sh** was crazy!

"I thought his name was Shaheed," I said, trying to keep my tone even.

I didn't want them to see that I was totally flustered. The agents glanced at each other. Then they looked back at me. Attempting to read me, and all the while trying to figure out whether or not I was being truthful. The reality was that I was telling the truth. I couldn't believe it. I was pregnant, in love, and in a relationship with someone I didn't know at all.

"Ms. Stanton, do you have any idea what's going on here, or who you're involved with?" the detective finally asked. I sighed in resignation, burst into tears, and said. "No, obviously I don't!"

Minutes slowly turned into hours, and my whole life changed in seconds. I felt as if I was inside of the movie 'The Matrix.' It was obvious that I had taken the wrong pill. I was anxiously waiting for someone to wake me up on the other side. This dream was the worst nightmare I'd ever had. I had no choice but to listen as they shared horrific details of alleged murder cases they had against the man I loved. The man I didn't really know at all. They explained how all the witnesses in the cases against him disappeared or ended up dead. And they pointed out to me that every time they pinned him for murder, he somehow manage to beat the case.

I had heard the stories about Shaheed on the streets, true enough. Hearing it on the streets and hearing it from a federal agent were two totally different things. Sh** got real, quick-fast, and in a hurry after that. It didn't get any realer than this.

I was aware of his notoriety, but I knew nothing about Shaheed's actual business. I really got offended that these detectives were questioning me about him. If Shaheed had committed all the murders they claimed, and witnesses were disappearing, then what in the hell made them think that I was interested in becoming one of those witnesses?

"Sir, I'm sorry, but I don't know anything about a hit out on a federal agent. I did not even know his name was Leonard," I said in tears.

I was an emotional wreck by then. My thoughts were in anguish and there was no avenue of escape. My situation was dire, I was pregnant and stuck in jail. And now I was finding out that my pregnancy was caused by a man I didn't even f**king know. It was obvious to me that Shaheed was a man who had been living a double life.

Was this sh** real? At this point my mind was in a state of conflict. The denial in me was fighting with my sense of realism. I was confused, overwhelmed, and felt betrayed. It was just too much going on at that moment. I just needed to pray. Pray and go to sleep. Maybe when I wake up this will all be resolved. I'll be able to climb out of the rabbit hole.

I awoke the next morning, and realized to my dismay that I was still stuck in this horrible place and the nightmare was far from over. No matter how hard I pinched myself, and pleaded for my Lord and Savior to come to my rescue, I was still trapped. The law had caught me inside a maze of illegal activities with no way out.

The federal agents' interrogation from the day before, replayed

nonstop in my mind. I had to digest all the facts and the pictures they had showed me. While strategizing and reliving my relationship with Shaheed over and over again, I was connecting all dots. I had to figure out how I was going to explain all this to my unborn child.

Maybe it was my sense of helplessness, but something about this dreadful situation pushed my mind back to the horror story my father and mother told me repeatedly throughout my life. It was one of the most shocking murder scenes which occurred in Buffalo, N.Y. The gruesome incident happened in 1978, and my family couldn't get away from it. It made headlines throughout the east coast. No matter what television channel you turned to, it was on. And for the next several years, this terrible incident was the talk of the town. It left a bitter taste on the lips of my family members.

October 31, 1978, was the day my first cousin, Gina, was violently murdered. It was a day that my family will never forget. At eleven years old, Gina was the prettiest child anyone would dare see. Her perfect milk, chocolate skin was accented by almond shaped eyes, and she had the perfect button shaped nose. Gina was a ballerina, and I was told how much she always loved me. My mother often told me that I was Gina's baby. Gina ironed my clothes, fed me, bathed me, and played with me. I was only a year old at the time of her death. My mom, my dad, my brother, my Aunt San, my cousins Gina and Kevin, and I all lived in the same two-family house located on 27 Girad Street. We were a very close-knit family and nearly all of us were raised in this home.

It was on a condensed street in Buffalo, New York. All the houses were right next to each other, separated by no more than six feet of yard space. If a fire was started in one home, the entire neighborhood would be burned down. On any day you could open your window and hear what your neighbors were watching on television. The houses were built the same way. They had the same height, foundation, and structure. They were just painted in different colors.

The father of my aunt's children, Lonzia Moss, practiced martial arts. He was a black-belt karate expert, who had perfected the art of his choice. Then one day he snapped, and decided that he was not only going to just kill himself, but take out everyone he had brought into this world.

My father was at work, but the rest of the family was home on this fateful day. All of a sudden there was a loud knock on the door. Lonzia stood outside the door. He wanted to take his children to eat at McDonald's. No one was aware of the shotgun he had hidden at the side of the house. My cousin Kevin, nine years old at the time, was asleep in the bed next to my brother, Lee. Even though Kevin was awake, Gina was the first one out the door. Then Kevin followed behind her.

It was over as soon as she stepped off the porch. Gina was shot once in the chest with a double-barrel shotgun. She was murdered by the man who had given her life! She was fragile and her body could never survive a blow of that enormous magnitude. As her life was blown away, Kevin wasn't given a chance to react. His father's gun ran out of bullets, but that didn't stop the deranged killer. With the butt of the murder weapon, Lonzia beat his nine year-old son, Kevin, into a coma.

Aunt San, my dad's younger sister, ran out the door with every bit of courage she could muster. Knowing she was no match for a black-belt, oh God, she put up a brave fight. Those were her babies! The man she once shared love with broke the shotgun on her face. Then he left the woman who had given birth to his children critically injured. She was lying in her own pool of blood right next to her children. My mother fought him off. Surprisingly she wasn't harmed, but he wasn't there to hurt her. Then the coward ran off before anyone had a chance to torture him.

When my father returned home, Gina's mangled body was still lying in the driveway. His niece was dead, his sister, and nephew were critically injured. My mother lost it, my brother was taken to a neighbor's house, and I was at the window watching, but I was unable to talk about what I had witnessed. I wasn't old enough to understand what I had witnessed. Or was I?

I have often wondered if something followed me from my dreaded past. How and why did Shaheed end up in my life? And now my child, just like my cousin, Gina, was to be the child of a psychopath? The similarities were mind boggling. Shaheed was a black-belt. He was a master of his art of choice. It was no secret that he could kill with his bare hands.

Would he ever do what my cousins' father did? I instantly felt a connection with my aunt, and started wondering how our lives placed us on similar paths. One thing was for sure. I decided then and there that I would learn from Aunt San's own experience. I was going to get the hell away while I still had a chance.

During the next forty-five days while waiting for my inevitable transfer to Clayton County Jail in Georgia, the last free moments of my life would constantly rewind in my mind. It left me thinking about what I could have done differently. I began wondering if Sheree told me everything she knew. Did she set me up? What was E thinking? Did he believe I set him up when he was told to return to the hospital? Who was giving these agents all the information? Why was I being questioned in Tennessee about Shaheed, when we both resided in Georgia? How did they know about my involvement with Shaheed? Was Phaedra going to stick to her word about representing me? Was I going to be out before my baby was born?

The bevy of questions was rampant. There were just so many possibilities rapidly running through my mind at one time. So many questions left unanswered, not even I could provide an answer. I couldn't find peace anywhere. The desperation of my situation constantly haunted me.

I was an emotional wreck by the time the date of my transfer had rolled around. The ride from Tennessee back to Georgia was long overdue. Even though I was still incarcerated, at least I was closer to my family. I was also getting closer and closer to my due date. Being transferred to Clayton County came with some rewards. If I did have the baby while I was incarcerated then my mother could come right to the hospital, and pick her up. The jail was only fifteen minutes away from my mother's home so I would have visitation every week. Yes, I will say that I thought I had the whole thing figured out.

It happened like clockwork. Every week, my mother came to visit me. Just like any good mother, she was at all my court appearances supporting

me one hundred percent. I had been in Clayton County Jail for nearly two weeks now, and it seemed like no one could get in touch with Phaedra. She was avoiding every person that tried to contact her on my behalf. All the calls to her personal cellphone and home number went unanswered and were never returned. So I had my cousin, Scott, call attorney, Ronald Freeman's office on a three-way phone call from jail. I spoke directly to Ronald myself.

"Ron, what's up with Phaedra? I mean she is avoiding all my calls when she knows what's going on with me. I don't know what is about to happen, but I know she promised to represent me. Now, she doesn't want to answer the phone," I said.

Ronald Freeman was well aware of the criminal activity that existed between Phaedra and me. Phaedra Parks shared an office with him on Spring Street. I knew for a fact that he definitely did not want to be implicated in any kind of way. Ronald briefly placed me on hold. Moments later, Phaedra was speaking with me on the phone.

"Phaedra what's up?" I yelled arrogantly.

She promised to visit the next morning. I hung up then waited. The next morning when she arrived for the visit, Phaedra went on and on about how we needed to let the air cool down. She told me that she had not forgotten about me, and promised that I would get out of this situation. I was facing four felony counts of forgery in the first degree for the transferred car titles in Georgia.

Auto Theft Detective, Pete McFarland, made sure he showed up at every hearing or court date that was scheduled. Phaedra promised me that everything would be over before I knew it. She gave me her word that she would look after my family if things went sour. Phaedra also explained and decreed that if anything happened to her, we would all lose. That was already understood. I said, "Just get me out of here Phae! I got to get home to my babies."

In the courtroom, I stood handcuffed and shackled. My big belly was protruding and bumping into anything in its way. My hair was nappy and braided straight to the back. My mother and Aunt Carrie sat inside the courtroom that day. They watched and listened as Phaedra pleaded our case. She was a great attorney, and did try her best, but what the hell happened to her influence? And what happened to the secret society amongst lawyers and judges? Superior Court Judge Matthew Simmons sentenced me to serve five years in the state penitentiary. I watched my mother fall to her knees. I broke my mother's heart that day. She cried like a baby as the Sheriffs led me away in handcuffs. My big belly and all walked out of there. That was it!

I was startled by the fact that I was going to give birth to my baby in prison. From that moment on, I made it my only concern to cherish every moment with my unborn child. I talked to her, and I read to her. I would sing to her while I rubbed my belly. I knew I would have to give her up at birth, but I wanted her to at least remember my voice. Five years sounded like a lot, but I knew I wouldn't have to serve the full sentence of five years. I had committed a non-violent crime. In the case of non-violent crimes, every day you served earned you three days toward your sentence. That meant I would only serve eighteen months.

My mother did not know that. I can't imagine how much she was stressing about my five-year sentence. She was thinking that her baby was gone for one thousand eight hundred and twenty five days. It wasn't the case and I couldn't wait to get back to the housing unit so that I could call and calm her nerves.

Unfortunately, the process would take at least six hours. Although all prisoners were housed in the basement of the courthouse, we would not be transported back to the housing units until each and every prisoner saw the judge that day.

My hips hurt, my back ached, and I was constantly in severe pain. The baby's weight in addition to my own weight was all pressed up against a cold hard steel bench. This was just too much and proved to be unbearable. Jail was made to be uncomfortable and they have definitely managed to pull that one off without a hitch!

Lying down on my right side with my belly hanging over the bench, I had a roll of tissue under my head serving as a pillow, and the uniform that I was wearing was my only cover. Cold air was blowing from the vents. The four concrete walls connected to a steal door reminded me of being in a dungeon every time it was opened and closed. This was nothing short of modern day slavery. It is what it is.

My meals consisted of two bologna sandwiches, one pack of mustard, warm milk, and a hard sour orange. I had to force myself to eat in the same cell with the crack-head who had just got off of a thirty-day smoking spree. Keep in mind that everything was inside the cell, including the toilet. She smelled like rotten flesh. Now she had all day to take a dump, but she decided to wait right good until I was about to eat to do so. My baby and I both nearly starved while I was incarcerated. I just couldn't eat in there! I was always nauseated. I'd be absolutely sick to my stomach.

I began to mentally prepare myself for this latest journey I was embarking upon. I had been to prison before so it wasn't that bad for me. This time was way different however. I had never given birth while I was incarcerated. Here I was again, sitting on their metal benches, and lying on the thin mats. The conditions were trying enough, but I knew I could get past that. What I didn't know was, how to get over the separation from my newborn baby. I had already been shopping for her before I was arrested. She had everything she needed. Shaheed was in contact with my mother as he awaited the birth of his child. If our daughter needed anything else, then he would be there to provide for her.

I hadn't seen Shaheed since I left that morning with E on the way to Tennessee. We were due for a visit. Seeing him again was different and difficult. I didn't feel the same about him anymore. My mind kept flashing back to the night my cousin Gina was murdered, the entire time we were having a conversation. My eyes stayed focus on his hands. I stared at them wondering what lives they may have snuffed out.

That first visit with Shaheed was filled with mixed emotions. There were questions which he refused to answer. And it left no doubt in my mind that he was totally capable of all the allegations against him. I was so glad when I thought about the letter I had given to Phaedra a few months back.

About two months after I found out I was pregnant, I wrote that if anything happened to me, Shaheed did it. I told Phaedra to put the letter in her safe, and keep it. Just in case. She gave me her word.

When the visit with him ended, I was heading back to my cell, and my water broke on the steps after leaving the visitation area. I could definitely attribute that to the high level of stress during that particular visit. I was taken down to the medical unit in a wheel chair. Then from there, I rode to the hospital in the back of the ambulance. All the while I remained handcuffed. I was afraid of whatever would come next for me, but once again, I refused to be fearful. I had no choice but to face up. This was my reality, but conflict reigned inside me.

May 31, 2004, rolled around. I would finally get to meet my baby girl. It should be a happy moment, but I dreaded the day. I was apprehensive, but was also looking forward to the birth of my child at the same time. I knew I wouldn't be able to care for my newborn. This occasion heralded my true calling from God. My right to raise my child was now being stripped away from me by man. I know we all have to be punished for our crimes. Lessons have to be taught, and we have to be reprimanded when we do wrong, but this was different. I felt I was experiencing something so wrong on all levels. But these things I know for sure.

I didn't kill anyone. I never molested anyone's child. And what made it all worse was I was the child who had been molested. How was I going to protect my baby girl? She can't speak yet. How could she tell me if someone had done her wrong? Think about this for a moment. It's natural for animals like bears and dogs to go insane if you attempt to separate them from their babies. How can man be so cruel?

Lying in the hospital bed on my back with one arm free, and the other handcuffed to the hospital bed, I was in pain. I was trying to lie on my side, but it was very, and I do mean very, uncomfortable. Somehow I managed to get through a most difficult labor. My eyes were bloodshot and strained watching the monitor, while listening to my baby's heartbeat. I was busy praying to God, asking that my baby would be okay. I prayed that I would be all right. I prayed that we would all eventually be okay.

Childbirth was supposed to be a joyous occasion, but this period had proved to be not only the longest nine months of my life, but also a very thorny time. My mind was swamped with musings. What was my baby going to look like? What about the bonding period between mother and child? How the critical first six weeks of me not being there would hurt my infant baby?

Yes, I had indeed been a street hustler, but I can tell you one thing, and anyone who knew me will attest to the same thing... I LOVE MY CHILDREN! I lived for them. I fought for them. Just like any other good mother, animal or human, I would have given my life for my offspring. In my present condition however, that was easier said than done.

Every other hour, the doctor checked my cervix to see how far I had dilated. Meanwhile, I was thinking about my mother, and how she was going to handle taking care of my other children along with my newborn. I didn't know how she was going to do it physically, and manage financially. I just knew she would find a way to get it done. Finally, the sheriff allowed me to

make that one phone call.

My mother answered on the first ring. Like always, she was most encouraging. She told me to put it in Gods hand, and not to worry. She said, "Don't worry about anything." The soothing sound of her voice calmed my fears, and assured me that my baby would be okay. Everything would be just fine when I made it back home. Now all I had to do was make it through this childbirth.

Delivering a child while handcuffed to a bed with a total stranger was painfully uncomfortable. For the record, it wasn't the doctor or midwife, but the sheriff who was there staring down at my vaginal area. His presence during such a private moment had to be one of the most difficult obstacles I had ever hurdled in my lifetime. That moment was also the most degrading experience in my life. I felt that his presence there was meant to destroy my humanity, kill my self-esteem, and murder my pride.

Turning her attention briefly to the sheriff, the midwife made a plea for him to leave the room. She asked, "Where is she going to run to? She has a seven-pound baby coming out of her butt!" The mid-wife was pleading, on my behalf, for compassion, but this disrespectful sheriff ignored her, and firmly continued to stand guard. He watched the entire childbirth process.

As the authority figure stared at me, I felt like a slave girl from the movie 'Roots'. This must have been the feeling that my ancestors had experienced during slavery. Maybe this was something I had just seen on TV. I don't know what it was, but it was a spirit that seemed all too real. The room was well lit, but still seemed so dark.

There was the midwife standing over me, instructing me to push harder. Realizing the delicate nature of the situation, she tried to be as comforting, and accommodating as she possibly could without jeopardizing her job. I wondered how she felt, and how many other times she assisted with the childbirth of some other lost, pregnant, incarcerated woman. How many times she had seen mother and baby separated.

"How much time will I have with her?" I asked.

"You get twenty-four hours, Ms. Stanton," the stern sheriff gruffly replied.

Tears rolled down my face, and I bawled like never before. I felt this treatment was unwarranted. My behavior didn't merit my baby being taken away from me. My baby didn't deserve to have her mother taken away from her. Why was this happening to me? Then my baby-girl came.

Seeing her for the first time was amazing. I could only thank God for my healthy, baby girl while looking in her big beautiful eyes. I kept praising God regardless of my circumstances. I still could not stop the tears of joy. This was mixed with plenty tears of sadness. I thanked God for her perfect body, and her perfect health. Once she was all cleaned up, the sheriff removed my handcuffs, affording me the honor of holding my newborn child.

"Emani Messiah," I whispered in her tiny right ear. I had already chosen her name. Emani, also spelled Imani, means faith and Messiah signifies the chosen one. She was chosen, and she did give me faith. Emani blessed me with enough faith to endure the road ahead, and make it back home to not just to her, but to all of my children.

I did not get to sleep a wink after the birth of my baby. It seemed as if I watched the big round black and white clock on the wall every minute it ticked. It was the same type of clock that hung on the wall in the many schools that I got expelled from. I sat there hoping and wondering if I could slow down the hands of time just this once. I held my baby close to my heart, sang in her ear, and told her how much I loved her. I told her that mama was going to come home soon. Hopeful that my voice would soothe her, and tide her over just as my mother's voice did for me.

The more I held my baby, the more I cried. All the nurses, doctors, and other patients walking by my room could hear my cries. I was told several times that if I didn't calm down, they'd take the baby back to the nursery. I heeded their requests every time, but as soon as I calmed myself down I started back up again. I just couldn't help it. The harder I tried to hold it in, the worse it got. I was pitiful.

No one came and took her from me even though they had threatened to do so. Most of the staff members on duty that day were made up of women. Deep down inside somewhere, I believe they understood what I was going through. I did the only thing I could. I prayed, cried, and held my baby. I was feeling hopeless and helpless. I watched the clock while closely holding my baby. I performed my motherly duties and changed her pampers. I kissed her often, in an attempt to soothe my precious infant. For the entire night I'd keep my eyes on the clock. I had to treasure every second, every minute, every hour. I had no idea how big she would be the next time I laid eyes on her.

It had been twenty-four hours, and it was time to call my mother again to let her know she could come to the hospital and pick up the baby. She must have snapped her fingers to get to the hospital. Twenty minutes later, she was standing outside my hospital room. My mother was excited to see me, but more excited by the presence of her granddaughter.

Our visit was short and sweet. It was about ten minutes to be exact. Once the time elapsed, my mother picked up the baby then was instructed to leave. I too would be leaving, but I would be handcuffed, and escorted to a patrol car. My mother had only one simple request.

"Please let me leave before her, I can't stand to see her in handcuffs" she begged the officer. They granted her request, and let her leave first before putting me in handcuffs.

With tears dripping from my eyes, I silently watched from the back window of the patrol car. Seeing how my mother took caution in strapping my beautiful baby girl into the back of her car brought me some relief. I could breathe a little better now even though I was still in captivity. There was a sense of reprieve.

I was headed back to jail, not going home with my baby girl, and as a mother, my situation made me feel like I was a complete failure. At least my baby girl was in my mother's care. There was some sense of satisfaction watching my mother's car driving away. She was the one person who could love my baby, and she now had her. My mother would love my baby girl just like she loved me. Tears were still welling. I felt like sobbing aloud. Without uttering a sound, my heart kept beating fast and with hope. Thank you sweet Jesus!

Chapter Seven
Finding My Way

"Stand at the crossroads and look; ask for the ancient paths, ask
where the good way is, walk in it, and you will find rest for your souls."

Jeremiah 6:16 (NIV)

Thinking of going back to the cold, hard, dark, loud dungeon brought me back to the real world. The vacation was over and I really wasn't in any hurry to return to Clayton County Jail. I would soon miss the comforts of warm covers, and the plush mattress of my stay at the hospital. And I definitely could not forget the luxury of the warm, tasty meals that most certainly didn't get me nauseated. I mean their food actually looked like food should be looking. No mystery meat!

Reality check finally bit me in the ass as soon as I returned to my

housing unit. My room was taken because the jail was overcrowded. I was issued a thin mattress, one sheet, and a thin blanket to make do with on the concrete floor.

I had just given birth and we were only allowed three pads a day. The pads were soaked and heavy from the blood caused by afterbirth. I was wearing three pads at a time. Since I had to get up and down off of the concrete floor repeatedly, the strain caused me to hemorrhage. I begged for more pads, but was denied any.

Blood was everywhere. In order to avoid bleeding on everything, I took one of my white T-shirts, and turned it into a pad. I had no other choice. Otherwise it would have looked like a crime scene. That was my only option.

I hand-washed the bloody white T-shirt inside the toilet. The water had enough chlorine in it to make my blood-soaked T-shirt white again. Stop turning up your nose. I just want you to know that at the time, there wasn't any other choice. It wasn't like I could send them out to the laundry. I did what I felt had to be done about my situation.

My breasts were sensitive and swollen with milk, but I had no baby with me to enjoy nature's nourishment. A mere breeze across my susceptible chest would cause extreme pain. The jail doctor had prescribed ice to help with the pain. One day, a guard walked by my cell, and caught me eating the ice. So she called down to the infirmary and cancelled my ice order. What a miserable bi**h! It was just another moment meant to destroy me, but I still couldn't understand how people could be so hateful. I was in my cell, not out in the open. Here was something she clearly could've overlooked. She didn't have the heart. I mean for heaven's sake I had just given birth!

My baby's crying tormented me every night. I kept hearing her tiny voice and that was pure torture in my head. I would caress my empty womb while milk oozed from my breast. It felt like I had just given birth to a stillborn child. I cried. Screaming, I hollered for my baby. I was locked up inside of a double prison. It felt like I was serving two sentences. I was inside four concrete walls and surrounded by the stockade of my own darkened mind.

I had lost everything important to me. Freedom was no longer mine it had been taken away. My possessions and children were all gone. The devil immediately began playing tricks with my mind. Fortunately, I knew that losing my mind was not even an option. The more I prayed, the stronger my mind became. I made a promise to myself, and I was going to weather this storm. Once more I was determined to make it.

Having given birth to my baby, the next thing to happen was getting shipped off to prison. I was impatient for that to happen because prison was much better than the jailhouse. Prison was more like an all female college campus. We all wore the same uniforms, but on this college campus we were surrounded by barbed wire fences, and under constant, strict surveillance. Freedom was not an option, but it was as close to a free living that a convict could ever experience.

At the all female prisons, the biggest difference was contact visits. This meant no more looking at my mother through a glass window, and most of all, I would be able to hold, and smell my baby. I longed for her. I begged my mother to contact the parole board, and get me shipped to prison. She

did. Two weeks after giving birth to Emani, I was packed up, and shipped to Metro State Prison.

On the first day, the correction officers had a field day with me. The moment I stepped off the bus, the correction officers constantly called me a repeater, and a clown. Perhaps that was all true. They did the name-calling as loud as possible, making sure everyone knew that this was my second trip to prison.

Little did they know that I wasn't fazed one bit. I was completely aware of their routine. The way they would get all up in your face, yelling and screaming. Correction officers would do everything in their power to provoke inmates into an ass-whipping. I just laughed at them and it would piss them off.

Finally, when they had enough of my contempt, they ordered me not to laugh. I stopped laughing, but kept that same sneer on my face. I wore the smirk just to let them know that I could care less about their nine-to-five. The fact was that I knew they were making pennies-a-day compared to what I had made.

From the same rules, to the same guards, same counselors, and the same routine, hardly anything had changed about the prison system. Before I was allowed to have visitors, I had to undergo diagnostics tests. This meant it would be at least four weeks before I could see my baby. That was cool because life was a little easier now. Three times a day during yard call I was able to mingle, and move around a bit. I could find out who was who. I was able to determine if I had any partners in here from the streets, and figure out who was affiliated with what.

I started networking to find out how I could immediately begin hustling, so that I could alleviate some of the stress from my mother. My first day on the compound, I ran into my home-girl, Gina. Her name was special. I always believed that my cousin, Gina, was my guardian Angel, always watching over me after she died. My cousin loved me so much I refused to believe that she ever left me.

However this Gina was my home-girl, and she worked in the prison kitchen. Everybody in there knew my rep on the streets, and in prison. I wasn't a crab, meaning nothing about me spelled selfish. I would give help to anyone who needed it. That meant even if it was my last dime. I never looked forward to being repaid. My blessings always came from above.

Gina hooked me up with some of everything like onions, cheese, taco meat, and cucumbers. It crossed my mind a couple of times why the cucumbers were in such high demand. But hey, who was I to judge?

Just in case you were wondering why I would be excited about those things. I would like to let you know that those items were hot commodities in prison. I could sell them to other inmates for commissary items. The taco meat was used to put inside of beef ramen noodles. The cheese was used for grilled cheese sandwiches. This was made by using a brown paper bag, and the dorm iron. Onions were used to add flavor to any food of choice. It would be a whole week before I could make commissary, but thanks to Gina, I was good.

Gina was serving a life sentence for murdering her husband. We

came to prison together on my last trip in, and Gina didn't have a dime to her name. I looked out for her and whenever I ate, she ate. She had a lousy husband that beat her for twelve years, and Gina wore the scars as best she could. She wasn't the prettiest thing to look at, and she did smell like onions sometimes, but I knew she was a person just like me. I wasn't afraid of her, and I didn't judge her. I couldn't judge her. She committed a crime and I committed a crime, and both of us were together in the same, exact prison. That was why the saying, "Don't burn your bridges..." proved to be true.

Diagnostic testing was a procedure all inmates went through when they entered the prison system. They are tested mentally and physically. After all the tests are completed, they are shipped to the prison that best accommodates their needs.

I remember standing in the long hallway with all the other females. Inmates after inmates were lined up against the wall, waiting to see the doctor. Prison was a male doctor's paradise. Many of the girls actually enjoyed lying on the table, spreading their legs wide, and letting the doctor's fingers play inside their exposed vaginas.

This was Dr. Feel Good for the inmates, and he knew exactly what he was doing. Despite giving birth to four other children in the free world, I had never ever had an OB/GYN doctor touch me on the inside with his fingers, the way that prison doctor did during my medical examination. What the doctor did that day caused me to relive the molestation I suffered when I was five years old. There was absolutely no protection.

When it was over, I jumped off the table and asked, "Did you enjoy it?" He nonchalantly smiled without saying a word. Pulling up my pants, I angrily stomped out. Before leaving the area, I silently made a note of how many girls were lined up waiting to see him. I observed that there were sixty-seven more vaginas for this pervert to violate.

The situation caused me tremendous sadness and made me very angry. All the female prisoners knew it was an issue of discontent, but were well aware that there wasn't a damn thing we could do to rectify it. Girls would gather around the yard during yard-call, and openly discuss the doctor's actions. There were some prisoners who enjoyed it, but others, myself included, felt violated.

The days were repetitive and time stopped for no one. I woke up every morning at five. I had my portion of the room cleaned, my bed made, and I would be standing by the side of my door at six for headcount. I passed all my tests with flying colors. I got word that I was on the list for Pulaski State Prison.

All the girls wanted to go to Pulaski because there were two-man rooms versus four-man rooms. Also Pulaski had bathtubs. Most prisons are equipped with standing showers only. I hadn't bathed in a tub in four months now. Pulaski was all right with me. I knew I would be going to Pulaski State Prison I just didn't know when I was to be transferred. All my testing had been completed, and I had visitation the upcoming weekend. I could see my mother and all of my children. I was just so excited and anxious anticipating the upcoming weekend.

I drew pictures for my children and colored them in with M&M's.

We didn't have crayons, so I improvised. I had a cherry sucker that I had gotten from one of my prior counseling sessions. I saved the piece of candy for Emani. I felt like I had to give my children something, anything to show them that I loved and appreciated them.

Although incarcerated, I still felt the need to provide for them anyway I could. My motherly instincts didn't just take flight along with my freedom. Through my childbirth experience with Emani, I had actually found a hidden well of love for my children. Thinking about them gave me pure joy.

The weekend finally arrived, and I heard my name called over the loudspeaker for visitation. I looked in my plastic mirror, and fixed my hair as best as I could. That meant without curlers or a hot iron.

I really could care less how my hair looked anyway. I just couldn't stop smiling because I had waited with tremendous longing for this moment to arrive. I skipped all the way to the visitation hall. I wanted badly to run, but running wasn't allowed on prison grounds.

Once I made it to the door of the gymnasium, I could feel my tears beginning to flow. I was actually going to hold my baby. The baby I hadn't seen since birth. I was burdened with thoughts of my daughter. Would she know me? Would she recognize me or the sound of my voice? Would she know I was her mother? She was almost two months now. Besides the fact that I was about to see her again, I wasn't sure of anything else.

My mother sat at the table smiling with Emani in her lap while my three boys, Lekwaun, Leontae, and Jayvien sat around the table smiling, and looking overjoyed. The wonderful joy of seeing their mother was overwhelming to all of us. They were just as excited about seeing their mother as I was about seeing my mother. Walking as fast as I could, I quickly reached the table and took my seat. I was so happy to see my children.

You would think they were happier than me if you could have seen the looks on their faces. I hugged my boys, and played with them first so they wouldn't feel neglected. The entire time I played with them I kept my eyes on Emani studying her up and down. My eyes were watching and I was feeling each breath she took. She was so pretty.

Holding Emani gave me an incredible feeling. I felt the way Celie, from the Color Purple, did when she saw the white woman in the store with her daughter, Olivia. Silently, I kept thanking God for reuniting me with my baby, I was missing her. I only wished that I could watch every breath she took. I wanted her to know and understand that my love for her was strong, and I would fight for her until my dying day.

Emani knew who I was. At least I believed she did. I couldn't blink because she stared at me so intensely. No matter what I did she wouldn't take her eyes off me. If she could speak, I was almost certain she would be asking, "Where in the world have you been?"

Brimming with excitement, I was overcome with joy. My long awaited opportunity to change my daughter's pamper had finally arrived. I knew she was in good hands, but I just needed to see my baby close-up. Holding my baby-girl close while examining her from head to toe, caused me to marvel at her perfection. She was so beautiful. I held her for what seemed like the entire visit, and I especially had her in my arms while I prayed,

"Thank you God for reuniting me with my children, especially my baby."

My mother silently watched me interacting with my children. With an occasional smile on her face, she appeared to be happy on the surface. However, I knew my mother very well and I could tell something important was weighing heavy on her mind. Maybe she was just waiting for the right time to let it slip. After we had sat around for about thirty-five minutes, my mother let her thoughts known.

"Angela, my money was low last week, and I called Phaedra to see if she would help me with pampers for the baby. You already know, I never heard back from her! And by the way, they got Shaheed!" My mother suddenly blurted.

"Who got Shaheed?" I asked. I knew he was into so much, and tied to so many things that I wasn't sure if he had gotten arrested or was it murder.

"The police have him. He's been charged with murder!" My mother answered wryly.

I stared at her briefly then redirected my focus on my baby. This was surreal and I just didn't know how to react to the news. Should I be laughing or crying? It was total confusion to say the least. I mean, what do I tell my baby?

My baby was born in a prison, and both her parents were imprisoned. I felt like I had already failed her. It was as if I had already deprived her of her shot at a real life. She was only two months old, and already had strikes against her. Oh Lord, please don't let her grow up to be like her mother, a victim of her own circumstances, I silently prayed. Needless to say that this new development stayed on my mind, and cast a dark cloud over the visit. The rays of light came from me seeing my children, and being with my mother.

The fact that Phaedra ignored my mother didn't surprise me whatsoever. Lately, she had been acting real sketchy anyway. I could tell she didn't want to be bothered. I had been calling her collect as well, and she never accepted my calls. I had dialed her home number so much I thought I would never forget it. But eventually I did. When I stopped calling her, she would write, sending me letters and pictures of her and Bobby Brown in the courtroom.

I would show her photos to my fellow-inmates. The celebrity snapshots brought me respect. All of a sudden other inmates wanted to be my friend because of my affiliation with a lawyer who represented all the stars. However, I would have preferred that Phaedra helped my mother out every once in a while. I really didn't need her photos. I knew exactly how Phaedra looked on the inside.

Chapter Eight
A Sorrow Heaven Cannot Heal

"Jesus wept." John 11:35 (NIV)

3 a.m., and I was awakened to the sound of the guard calling my name over the intercom.

"STANTON, PACK IT UP," he yelled.

This meant that I was being shipped to my permanent housing unit at Pulaski State Prison. I would serve the rest of my time there. There was some reservation in leaving Metro State Prison. It was located in Atlanta, and this made it easier for me to have visits with my children. All my collect calls were local, and weren't as bad on my mother's phone bill. In retrospect, I was ready to go. Being transferred to another prison meant I was getting closer to finishing my time and returning home.

Quietly, I jumped out of bed so I wouldn't disturb my cellmates. It wasn't that I was scared, but I did this out of respect. In prison, one wasn't classified by the crime you committed. One could be sleeping next to a mass

murderer and not be aware of it. The only way one would know, was if that person revealed the information to you. Sometimes this person's crime could be shown on the news, or maybe people from their hometown told you about it.

There were plenty of baby killers on the inside. I would stare at them just wondering how they could harm a precious and innocent human being. I would never let them catch me looking. If they could kill their own baby, I could only imagine what they would try to do to me. Don't get me wrong, I would at anytime hold my own, but it was just always good to know what you were up against.

I packed up all my belongings, including my bible, toothbrush, two uniforms, three white panties, three white bras and a couple photos. Everything was folded, placed neatly inside my pillowcase, and thrown over my shoulder. I walked to the front gate along with the other thirty-five women being shipped out with me that day. Then we waited. I waited in the twilight of the early dawn as the morning dew fell and tickled my face. It sure felt good too. I hadn't been out at that time of morning in what seemed like ages.

We were all cuffed together by our wrists and ankles. One by one we were escorted onto the bus, walking carefully to avoid falling on our faces. That would have caused a domino effect. I tried not to watch as we left civilization, but something made me do it. Something made me watch as the life I knew faded away. I was uncertain of my future and not sure of what the near future had in store for me. I was leaving known territory to dwell in a dry, desolate place.

The trip to Pulaski State took nearly three hours. I got tired of looking out the window, and grew sick of watching the free world pass me by. Cars with family drove alongside the bus and I wished it was me driving the car. There were children in the back seat laughing and playing. It made me think of my family, and I decided that just as long as my children were with me I would be good. It didn't matter as long as we were a family, and we were together. Unfortunately, that wasn't my life anymore. I wondered how old my baby would be when I had the chance to live life freely again.

We had just arrived and I was homesick already. The air was different. I mean you knew without a doubt that you were in prison. The yard had to be one of the biggest I had ever seen. It appeared to start at one end of the earth, and stretched to the other. Barbed wire fences surrounded us and Georgia red clay covered the land as far as you could see.

There were so many girls passing by. Face after face, each and every one of their faces told a different story. I eventually lost count, but somehow I found the time to scan each and every one. I needed to observe my new confines. I was in the jungle, and with that being said I knew that only the strong survived in this place.

This was my home for now. No matter how much I screamed, cried, or begged for mercy, there was no turning back at this point. I kept thinking about my mother and Phaedra, and all those pep talks they had given me in the free world. How could I apply them to my current situation?

My mother always said, "You can't change your past, but you can control your future." That was my favorite one. But what do you do when your past was always haunting you?

I had been there for three days and realized that Pulaski State wasn't as bad as I thought it would be. Even if it had been, I would've had to make the best of it. I called home once a month. It seemed like a long time between calls but each call helped my time go by faster. Every time I spoke with my mother and my children it gave me strength. Hearing about Emani and how she was growing always brought a smile to my face. When I spoke with my mother on the phone Emani would be in the background speaking her baby-talk as loud as she possibly could. It was the most beautiful sound I could've ever heard.

Sitting in the day room, I was watching music videos with my bunk-mate. I was shocked when I saw Jay on B.E.T. Young Jeezy! I didn't even know he could rap. Jay had always been a mild mannered considerate person. He was a hustler just like me. My hustle was white collar types and his hustling was the ones he rapped about. He was now becoming a major star.

Jay and I had met back in '98 at the Spot Light Night Club in Macon, Georgia. The clubs in Macon were always jumping. If it wasn't the Spot Light, then it would be G Money's. And after partying like a rock star at the club, many nights it would be Jeezy and I getting down.

My mother was a pastor at a church in Macon, called I AM Ministries. Macon was only an hour and fifteen minutes from Atlanta, depending on how fast you drive. I made frequent runs up and down Interstate 75 South traveling between Atlanta and Macon. A lot of those trips were to see Jay.

I wasn't his girlfriend. That was clear. It was just sex. We enjoyed each other's company so that made it more than just sex to me. I couldn't tell you how many nights I spent with Jay. It used to be me, my home-girl, Tina, Jay, and his homeboy, Ellerbee, or like we called him, Kinky B. You couldn't find one without the other. One of the good things about that set up was we knew how to have a good time.

Just in case you didn't know, Jay had money long before the world came to know him as Young Jeezy. Because of his hustle, Jay had mad respect on the streets. No matter what he did or what he was doing, he always found the time to bless someone. So I knew he would in turn be blessed. Our sex-capades, or rendezvous lasted well over three years. He knew all my friends and I knew his boys. He slept with a couple of my friends, and I did with a couple of his too. Hey, we were young. We had money and did whatever we felt like doing. That was before the fame came.

I won't go into too many details about our sex life. Like I said be-fore, Jeezy was a real good dude, and to me he was much bigger than just sex. He never once disrespected me, and never treated me like a freak or a whore. He would do anything he could to help another person. For those reasons alone, I still have the utmost respect for Jay.

Instant happiness and genuine excitement was what I felt for Jay when I saw him doing his Young Jeezy rap on TV. Every time I did, I ran to

the phone, and had one of my cousins on the end verify that I knew Jeezy. Not only that I knew him, but we had relations and all.

The women locked up in prison with me had to be living inside a box their entire lives. They actually refused to believe that it was possible for me to personally know someone on television as famous as Young Jeezy.

Seeing Jay on TV while I was in prison actually did something for my spirit. It gave me hope and inspiration. I was so glad to see that he was doing well. He was smart and had done the intelligent thing. He had taken his money and turned it into something. If someone that close to me, someone who I had been with, someone from my own hood had made it, so could I.

My life at this point was manageable. I had gotten myself into a routine, and if I kept it up all of this would soon be over. My life would eventually be back to normalcy. I was looking forward to being back at home with my children, my mother, my grandmother, and family.

It became habitual for me to be waking up at five every morning. I would be showered, dressed, and clean my room by seven, in time for chow. Then I would go to the chow hall, and be back in my cell, waiting on the guards to do headcount. After headcount, I would report to my detail. I worked in laundry room, and probably washed and folded over two thousand uniforms per day. At three-thirty in the afternoon my detail was over. I would report for chow by five. Then after the second headcount conducted at six in the evening, I would be in my cell either reading or writing until I fell asleep. At least that was the plan.

November 16, 2004, was a day that changed my life forever. I was six months deep into serving my sentence. Then I had the most vivid and realistic dream about my mother the night before. In my dream I was standing at the doorway of an apartment, watching my mother walking up the sidewalk. She was carrying three buckets. Then she walked right past me and went inside the house. There were three aquariums sitting in the middle of the living room floor. I closely scrutinized my mother emptying the contents of the three buckets into one of the aquariums. My mother handed me a net. I watched through the glass as an assortment of tropical fish frantically swam back and forth. They were trying to absorb their new environment.

One particular fish caught my attention. While observing this beautiful creation my mother said, *"Take the net and separate the fish."* I grabbed the net, and began reaching for the fish I had observed previously. The net wasn't long enough to reach the bottom of the tank where the fish was swimming.

I stuck my arm in the water right along with the net. Before I knew it, a snake was swimming toward my hand. I tried pulling my arm out of the tank as fast as I could, but it was too late. The snake had sunk its teeth deep into my skin, and then swam off.

My mother examined the bite mark. Then she kissed the area of impact, and like magic, it healed instantly. She looked at me and said, *"Angela!"* Once she was certain she had my undivided attention she continued, *"Honey, you had no business with your hand all the way in the tank. That's*

why I gave you the net. If you hadn't had your hand in the water he wouldn't have been able to bite you. Therefore you have to come out from amongst thee and be ye separate." She then shook my head with her hands to make sure I understood. *"You have to come out from amongst thee and be ye separate. That's the only way you're going to make it. You got it?"*

"I got it ma," I replied. Then just like that she had disappeared.

I was instantly awoken from the dream, only to fall back asleep moments later. This time an angel awoke me. Lying on my back asleep, I felt the warmth of a mother's touch rubbing my chest. I was awaken by the touch and encountered an angel floating on the right side of my bed. The angel was the most beautiful thing I had ever seen.

She looked just like some kind of a fairy, except I could see right through her. She was a purplish-blue color, and was glowing. The angel said to me, *"Angela honey, it's time for you to wake up!"* I looked over at the clock and it was five a.m. It was the same time they woke us up every morning. I looked back for the angel, and she was gone. I was overcome with joy and a sense of peace that surpassed all understanding. This was my first encounter with a heavenly being. The whole ordeal confirmed that God was really in my life!

Jumping out of bed, I had the entire room cleaned. I couldn't wait until they turned the phones on so that I could call my mother, and tell her about my dream along with my encounter of such a pretty angel. I was so fascinated by the unknown. I always had been, but I wondered what the dream meant. After replaying it in my mind over and over again, I had kind of figured it out in my head.

My dream meant exactly what she had said, "Come out from amongst thee and be ye separate." It was time for me to step away from anything, and everything negative.

I remember sitting in the dorm hall at a table with three other women who were from my dorm. We were all enjoying a board game of 'Life'. I was the pink car. Ever since I could remember, the pink car always had to be mine. It was my lucky car. Even as a little girl over at my Aunt San's, playing with my cousin's Maurice, Man-Pan, and Jo-Jo, I always had the pink car.

If I couldn't have the pink car I wouldn't play. I wasn't compromising, sorry. As we played the board game I imagined how my life would have been had I made different choices. Nobody ever went to prison in the board game. So really, losing the game was never an option. Everyone always won the game. Some just ended up with more money than others, but that was the board game Life, not real life.

I was just about to spin the wheel when I heard my name being called over the loud speaker.

"Angela Stanton report to the Chaplain's office..."

I was glad that my name had been called. This would give me a chance to get out of the dorm and enjoy some well deserved fresh air. Then one of the women playing the board game with me said, "No Angela! You

don't want to go to the Chaplain's office! Anytime they call you to the Chaplain's office it's always bad news!" I stared at her, and immediately the dream popped to the surface of my mind. Then I thought about the angel, and what she had said to me. *"It's time to wake up!"*

Instead of going to the Chaplain's office, I ran to the pay phone. I called my grandmother's home collect, and I could hear the despair in their voices as they accepted my call on the other end. I already knew that my mother was gone. I didn't even need to ask the question. My cousin, Donna, tried to tell me what I already knew, but she was too emotional, and could hardly speak. She just held the phone silently as I screamed for my mother.

"Donna please let me speak to my mother!" I said, after getting no response from her. The phone remained silent, but on the other end of the line, I could hear my grandmother crying through the phone. She was mourning for her baby.

"Donna… Do-o-o-n-n-n-n-a-a-a! Pl-e-e-e-a-a-a-s-s-e-e-e! Donna! Please let me talk to my mother!" In two simple words she replied, "I can't!"

When I regained consciousness, I was in the infirmary. My feet, knees, chest, and my wrists were bound. I kept trying to fall back asleep. "Please GOD! GOD pl-e-e-e-a-a-a-s-s-s-e! Please father NO! No-o-o-o-o-o! I want my mommy. My mo-m-m-m-y! OH GOD… NO!" My heart and soul pleaded, to no avail.

Every time I woke up, I wept uncontrollably until I cried myself back to sleep. I refused to eat, and drink. I just wanted to lie there! Lie there and die! My hopes were dashed. Life as I knew it was over. In the middle of the night during a deep sleep, I awoke to the feeling of breath in my ear, and I heard my mother's voice! *"Angela I'm with you! Angela I will never leave you! Angela I love you!"*

I jumped up. Well, I tried to jump up. I was further confined in restraining belts and chains, but I opened my eyes to the sound of her voice. She was nowhere to be seen. I never imagined that my mother would die while I was in prison. I was filled with the guilt of all my misdeeds. At this point it seemed as if everything was my fault. Had I been there for her, maybe things would have worked out differently. Why couldn't I be there for her now when she needed me the most...?

My mother was fifty-five years old when she lost her life to a massive heart attack. It fell on me like a ton of bricks. At twenty-seven years old, I was crushed by the weight of losing the only friend I had ever had. Lying on my back, I was feeling powerless by the thought that I couldn't be there for my mother. I couldn't be there for my children. Four concrete walls surrounded me and seemed to close in faster in more ways than I could ever have imagined. There was no one there to comfort me. I wasn't surrounded by any family member. I was totally and completely alone in a very cold, dark place. There was no light and no help came from anywhere. It was then that I felt God had finally forsaken me.

I was in the infirmary for three days, doped-up under medication. Whenever I came down from my high, I was forced to deal with the pain of

losing my mother. I cringed in the face of my reality, and could have stayed doped up forever, but I knew I was dying in that place. Every time I thought of any type of food, it would cause me sickness. All I could think of was my mother lying dead in the city morgue. Naked, her body would be stretched out on some cold, metal table. She was gone from my physical world and I could no longer communicate with my best friend.

Her flesh would rot, and the thought of her never being able to eat again made me sick. The problem was that there was no food inside my stomach for me to regurgitate. It proved to be a painful experience every time I went through a vomiting spell. I had cried so much, the salt from my tears burned my cheeks. I actually had scars on each side of my face left behind by my tears of pain.

My brother tried desperately to have me transported from the prison to my mother's funeral. When this didn't work, he had no choice, but to call Phaedra. This time she actually came through. At the time of my mother's death, my brother was committed to a professional basketball contract. He was drafted overseas, and had been playing in Italy since graduating from college. Lee had to make it home from Italy, bury our mother, and return overseas. This was a trying time for the both of us. She really was all we ever had.

There was a problem getting me transported to the funeral. Fulton County was under scrutiny because of the Brian Nichols case which had happened earlier the same year. He was the prisoner who had escaped while being transported. He had murdered a Judge, a court clerk, a deputy and a civilian. As a result, Phaedra was unable to get anyone from Atlanta to do a prisoner transport. After a couple of days, I was finally informed that my brother paid Gwinnett County to transport me. Phaedra knew a sheriff there who agreed to do the transporting.

The women incarcerated with me tried all they could to offer comfort. They washed and ironed my clothes for me and styled my hair to a cute pin up do. Although I was pretty on the outside, my insides were ugly. I totally ceased all communication with anyone and everyone. I didn't even want their comfort to be honest. They didn't know me, and I didn't want their hands on me. In my mind, I was really tripping HARD… And at times, I was known to have violent outbursts.

I felt remorse, guilt and shame all at the same time. I just didn't want to be bothered, and was having a hard time coping with reality. Practically on the verge of losing my own damn mind, I didn't know who to trust. I was giving everybody the side-eye.

Having flashbacks became a normal occurrence, and I was reverting to my former self. I was back to being that angry, hateful young girl I was before meeting Phaedra Parks. It was an ugly, dark demon I thought I had buried for good. I didn't want that spirit to rise back up. So I fought it. I accepted their gestures of kindness, but it didn't really matter to me. I had absolutely no reaction at all. I didn't have a clue as to what was going on. Nothing and I mean nothing, seemed real to me. I was in a total state of devastation and

shock. This was the worse heartache I had ever experienced. I didn't call back home and didn't speak to the guards at the prison. I didn't speak to any of the women locked up with me. The minute they all saw my face, they knew. The grim-reaper forewarned them. He had been by my doorsteps.

The funny thing was that a week earlier, I was standing in the chow-line when three of my dorm mates, or should I say 'fellow slaves' passed by me causing quite a commotion. In the middle of the other two, was a girl barely able to walk. Her name was Angela. Yes, she had the exact first name as mine. Angela was crying hysterically. So being the compassionate person that I am, I immediately offered my assistance. I asked, "What's wrong?"

She held her head up with all of her strength, looked me dead in my eyes and said, "My mother just died." Exactly one week prior to the death of my mother. I remembered thinking, God I couldn't imagine how she was feeling. What would I do if I were in her position? I thought to myself that this was just another sign from above. Seven days later, the reality of my fellow slave became mine.

Every word and every thought that came to mind made me think of the one person I had always depended on, my mother. Here one day, she was gone the next. It now seemed just that quick. Not only was I thinking of losing my mother, but now, what about my children? What would happen to them? Who would care for them? What about my baby, Emani? What about the promise I made to myself?

After I had been molested, I pledged that I would never allow the horrible experience to happen to any of my children. My mind was running a thousand miles-a-minute. My thoughts were never letting up, not once. There was no single moment of peace. I couldn't even begin to think straight. Nothing at all was making sense to me. I found myself now questioning God. Was there even a God? A God so merciful that he would allow one person to go through so much pain...? What was the purpose of our existence? Were we just born to die...?

When the Gwinnett County sheriff arrived to pick me up, it took me a long while to make it past all the barbed wires. With every step, it seemed like I was pat-down and searched. I was scanned with metal detectors as I passed through metal doors. Malnourished, dehydrated, I was left deprived of the ability to accurately think. I was moving slowly because I was feeling so weak.

It had been seven days since the day my mother left this earth, and I hadn't eaten one single crumb. I barely had enough strength to lift my feet from the ground. Gwinnett County officials handcuffed me, and I was placed in the back seat of their patrol car. Finally I would be going back to Atlanta, Georgia. Never in my wildest dreams had I ever imagined that I would be returning to attend my mother's funeral.

The trip was long, and heart wrenching. When I stepped over into

the back seat of the police car it seemed as if I had crossed over into another realm. The atmosphere was different. The air was so heavy. The Gwinnett county officers there to transport me looked like the enemy. They wore bulletproof vests, carried side-arms, Tasers, mace, and handcuffs, along with hog-ties. A shotgun was strategically placed on the front seat. This was done all for me, just in case I wanted to get stupid. I was too weak and couldn't think clearly.

It was a very dark gloomy day. The skies opened up resulting in a light drizzle. The rain from the sky appeared like tears and made the somber atmosphere even sadder. A reality I didn't want to face awaited my return. I hadn't thought about my other family members. All I could think about was my children, and having to stare death in the eyes from close up.

Remember all those times before when I told you I wasn't afraid? Well, that day I was scared to stare death so close in the eye. I would rather it had taken me and not my dear mother. Fear had its grip on me this time, and I couldn't shake it. I kept trying to hold on to whatever hope or life I had left. I didn't want to see death.

Death was cold! It ALWAYS showed up uninvited, and at the wrong time. It never comes in a peaceful manner. Death always leaves you with a feeling of emptiness. Nothing seemed worse than death. It was the one thing I knew you couldn't bounce back from.

During the whole ride back, I couldn't help but think of my mother. I thought of every word that she had ever spoken to me. Everything she tried to teach me. Every time she yelled at me for not listening when I should've. All the walks through hell that I had made her take. She had tried endlessly to help me wake up and smell the coffee. Slowly but surely, it finally dawned on me what the angel meant. It was time for me to wake up. She was telling me to wake up mentally and spiritually, not physically.

In my dream, my mother was leaving me with her last words. She was giving me her key tips for survival. She came back to me in a spiritual realm and no one could tell me it wasn't real. I know because I experienced it. You can't tell me I was so depressed that somewhere in my mind I believed. Oh no! I was not crazy. Save that. I knew exactly what was going on.

Arriving at Gwinnett County Jail was one of the worst things that could have ever happened to me. I would like to give you this straight. I stepped out of the back of the patrol car. A six-foot tall woman, wearing a size twelve boots, and tan jumpsuit. 'State Prisoner' was emblazoned across the back of my jumpsuit in big bold black letters. I must have appeared threatening. The female guards were acting as if they were very much intimidated by my presence. For all they knew, I could have been a mass murderer. That was exactly how I was treated. It was like I had killed a whole lot of people. I was slung up against the wall like an old mat. Then I was patted down for any weapons.

"Do you have any bobby pins in your hair?" A female guard sternly asked.

"Yes." I responded. "But, I need these for my mother's funeral in

the morning."

The bobby-pins in my hair were purchased from the inmates' store list in prison. I guess the word 'but' was considered my refusal to take out the bobby-pins. Although she never asked me to take them out, she just asked if I had any in my head.

Before I knew it, I was slammed on the floor, and the knees of three officers were in my back. I was firmly pinned between the officers and the concrete floor. I tried to understand why this was happening to me? Why the female guard yelled for back up?

When she dug her fingernails into my arm, I snatched my arm away from her and that was considered an assault. I didn't even consciously realize that I snatched my arm away from her. I was snatching my arm away from the pain her nails caused when they dug into my flesh.

They hog-tied me and left me face down in a pool of my own urine. I stayed in this position in a holding cell for the remainder of the night. The next morning I was untied, given a clean uniform, and told to clean up myself before the chief arrived.

When the chief came in, he asked me what happened. So I told him my version. He chose not to believe my story. I told him that I didn't even have the strength to fight. The only thing I wanted to do was to tell my mother goodbye. I was pleading my case to him.

The chief instructed the officers to place me in the back of the car so that we could head out. I tried fixing my hair back together after the guard had ripped out all of the bobby pins. I fixed my uniform, tucked my shirt in, and folded the bottom of my pants. I was visibly dehydrated and weak, but just wanted to get this behind me.

Two mean-faced, redneck officers placed me in the back of their vehicle, and we headed toward the expressway. I had no idea where my mother's funeral was being held, I just knew it was somewhere in Atlanta.

Watching every exit the officers drove by, I noticed that they weren't stopping. They transported me straight back to prison. When we pulled up, and I saw the prison gates, I was so angry. It was enough to push me over the edge and make me go crazy. What had happened was so ironic. It was such a simple misunderstanding that could've been easily corrected. But I knew then that it just wasn't meant for me to be there.

Seeing my mother dead, I wouldn't have been able to handle that. To watch my children mourn, not be able to hold them, and then return to prison would be unbearable. God knew best. It would've just been too overwhelming for me.

God knew that the look of death on my mother's face would have been enough to drive me insane. I couldn't cry anymore. My feelings were numb, and I just kept pinching myself, trying to wake up from the nightmare. At that very moment, I chose to believe that my mother was still alive somewhere, waiting for me to return.

Three days later, I received a sympathy card from Phaedra. She in-

formed me that she had to stand in place for me at my mother's funeral. She told me how beautiful my mother looked, and the unexpected high turnout. She elaborated, explaining how there were people lined up outside the church, waiting to pay their respects. The outpouring was tremendous. Phaedra had even given some of my grief-stricken family members a ride from the church to the gravesite.

"Be strong and everything will be great when you come home. God bless! Phaedra."

I read the letter a couple more times, and smiled in satisfaction. I knew my life was completely different now. My mother was laid to rest, and no longer dwelled amongst the living. Only thing was, I felt dead too. Riddled with guilt and buried in a bottomless pit of depression. I looked just like my mother.

The simple task of looking at my reflection, proved difficult. I went two months without ever looking in the mirror. I hated what I saw looking back at me from behind the glass. I hated what I had become. Three months after her passing, I finally mustered the strength to look in the mirror. I sat there staring, looking at the person in the mirror, and trying to figure out exactly who she was.

I wanted to know what, and why things happened the way they did. No person as a child have said, "When I grow up, I want to go to prison." What went wrong? Somewhere in my mind I figured that if I could get these answers, then maybe I could get to the root of the problem, and fix myself.

Replaying every event in my life that had a dramatic effect on me, I began a self analyzing journey. I saw the five-year-old girl who died that day when a much older cousin molested her.

Anthony was someone my family trusted. He was my mother's nephew. There were all those times I ran away from so much pain, not knowing I wouldn't be able to totally escape. This was an inexplicable kind of pain that existed deep inside. A silent hurting which traveled everywhere with me!

I relived the moments in time when my mother chose her husband over me. I saw the time going by when my father couldn't be my father anymore. I crossed paths with everyone who hated me, mistreated me, and spoke so many foul things of me. Those instances were the ones that turned me to the streets. I was out there in the cold world, searching for some type of acceptance. I had never felt needed or wanted by anyone.

The needs were still there, but in order to address them, I had to figure out my life. There was some soul-searching to be done. I had no sense of my true identity. I really needed to do something about what and who I had become. I refused to die after living the life of nobody.

Knowing everything I had gone through must be for a reason, I never regretted being born into this world an innocent child. I had just as much of a shot at living as anybody else. The one thing my mother always tried to point out to me was to never give up. She always told me that quitters never win.

All the pain I was going through, and all the suffering I did, had to be for some cause. But what? It seemed like the enemy was constantly play-

ing tricks on my mind. There was so much separation between mother and child that it left me detached from reality. First my mother and her child were separated. Then it was my baby and her mother. I had experienced it on both ends, and it wasn't a good feeling.

Only the strong survived, was what I kept hearing inside me. I knew that was a fact, and it was time for me to rise above my circumstances. I had to make it home to my five children, Aleea, Lekwaun, Leontae, Jayvien and Emani. They were the five perfect reasons to live, and not die. Losing was not an option. No time to ball up into a shell and depart this life. It was time to live, time to deliver, and time to heal. It was time to set my mind free!

I loved to write, and I found healing whenever I wrote about something. It was my way of releasing built up emotions inside me. There was something cathartic about letting another person hear my story or reading about someone else's misfortunes in life. This by some means made me grateful for the life I was living. I mean just the mere fact of knowing that you're not the only one—it helped. I needed an outlet for my pain, something to keep my mind active and focused. I was already preparing for my future. So I decided to write a book while I was locked up.

I knew that every woman inside the walls of this prison had a story. You didn't just trip over a rock, and land in prison. It was a process that brought you there. You were tried and proven guilty. I knew that. Just like me, none of them had planned from childhood to end up living behind prison walls.

We all wanted to be singers, actors, lawyers, or doctors, just like every other normal kid in the world. I really wanted to hear the stories. Not only did I want to hear them, but also I needed them documented. I had made up my mind that I was going to help young troubled girls. I too had once been labeled, 'Troubled'.

The one thing that I remembered from my childhood was all the counselors. Yes, they did all possess degrees in their fields, but they lacked real life experience. In my view, they weren't survivors. So how could they tell me how to overcome childhood sexual abuse, if they were never abused sexually as a child? I couldn't look up to them, and that was because I couldn't bond with them.

These girls nowadays need someone they can bond with, and look up to. If they look at me, and see I made it against all odds, surely they would believe and have faith that they too could make it through the darkest hours.

Every single day I was walking around Pulaski State Prison armed with a pen and several pads. And every day it was my goal to document someone's pain with as much fervor as I had when I walked around them luxury car lots, documenting information for Phaedra's scheme. I used some of the same skills, and documented information for the world.

This time my efforts were for the purpose of healing rather than causing harm. I was now doing more good than bad. In addition to that, I would be doing my part to help the world become a better place. As I interviewed my fellow prison mates, I never quite understood what it was about me that they trusted.

What it was about me that got them to open up, and share things about them that they would have never told anyone. I was going to use their stories to help young girls. Of course, these would be the type of young girls following in their footsteps. Or should I say, following in my footsteps. I had experienced pain so severe that I never want ANYONE to ever go through what I had been through.

Before I knew it, I had many stories. They were from so many different women of all walks of life. These women were of different races, different religions, different ages, and had committed crimes as petty as theft to crimes as serious as capital murder.

Hearing the story of how a fifteen year old girl was raped, and molested by her father her entire life, until she grew tired of his abuse, and shot him dead, gave me strength. When I heard the story of the young woman who learned she was HIV positive after being tested in prison, I could not for one moment understand how it felt to walk in her shoes.

It hurt me so much to hear their stories! I cried with them when I documented their truths. But I refused to let the pain I felt deter my efforts. I knew that someone somewhere needed to hear these stories. The first time a child tells me that I haven't been through what she had been through, I could turn to a page in this book, and find the story amongst the pages. A story that was true, and actually relatable existed in my collection. These were stories that would make any child think twice. It was my impetus to being a beacon of light in the dark world. This was the sole purpose of my writing, and I dubbed it crime prevention.

'Life Beyond These Walls', was my first book. It was written and completed during my imprisonment. All I had to do was keep all my pages together. I could present the book to Phaedra Parks. She had connections in the entertainment industry and maybe could help me kick it off. I also figured she would be proud of my accomplishment, seeing as though I did something useful with my time. Her connections were within the reach of a button. I knew I was a great writer. As long as I cut Phaedra in on the money then we would be good, and everybody could win. At least, that was how I saw it.

Being a convicted felon was hard enough. Let it not be forgotten that I was a single mom. With that in mind, I knew I had to become an entrepreneur. Not only would this book heal the masses, but it would also provide me with a way to financially care for my children.

I was already connected. I just had to get the book to Phaedra. I couldn't take the risk of sending it in the mail. She may never receive it. So I held onto it for dear life. I wanted to personally hand the written manuscript directly to her.

The next series of months were somewhat like my hibernation pe-

riod. My focus was on perfecting my book, and dreaming of the lives that it was going to touch, inspire and enrich. I began cleansing my soul. I began the process by forgiving myself, finding myself, and loving myself. Everything I had come to know was different.

By now, it had been four months since the death of my mother. I wrote to my family, they never wrote back. I made collect calls that were never accepted, and I pleaded for someone, anyone to bring my children to see me. After about four months my cousins, Connie and Donna finally brought my children down for a visit. I also received a card from my cousin, Kate, and a letter from my cousin, Sylvia.

My immediate family was very large. This fact was due to my maternal grandmother who had given birth to ten children. I came from a family of about seventy aunts, uncles, and cousins. I guess a letter from two relatives out of seventy isn't that bad. Hard times showed me who really cared for me. One relative who was always there was my dear, sweet Aunt San. She wrote me just about every two weeks without even knowing that she was saving my life.

No matter how hard I fought, no matter how loud I screamed, and no matter how much I cried, there was nothing in this world that I could do to bring my dear mother back. This was when I learned that I had absolutely no control over my life. I had to let go, and let God take over. I stopped worrying. I stopped stressing and started praying. Then I found the true meaning of stepping out on faith. I could no longer talk about it. I had to be about it.

Chapter Nine
My trail of tears

The LORD said to Satan, "Very well, then, everything he has is in
your power, but on the man himself do not lay a finger."

Job 1:12 (NIV)

Three months into my sentence at Pulaski state prison, and I was
called into the counselor's office. They notified me that I was being shipped
off to another prison. Lee Arrendale State Prison had just been converted
into a coed prison, and I was included in the first shipment of women to ever
reside there. This didn't pose a problem or a threat to me. I felt I was moving
into a different environment, and also moving closer to home.

Lee Arrendale was the biggest prison I'd ever seen. I thought Pulaski was big, but Lee Arrendale was much bigger. As a prisoner you walked
everywhere you went. At this facility, the only car you had the luxury of riding in was the patrol car. It was with certainty that prisoners rode in the back
seat. Walking was good though. I would be in great physical shape by the
time of my release. My new home consisted of nothing more than hills and

concrete. The staple diet was peanut butter and syrup sandwiches.

Getting acclimated and blending into my new surroundings was now my focus. I was living with an entirely new group of women, and I was in the midst of a whole new flock. These women didn't know me, and they didn't know my character. I didn't want them to get offended by my nonchalant attitude. Certainly I didn't need anybody thinking that I was a snob because I didn't play along with their games. There wasn't much time for games in this new existence. I had my whole life ahead of me.

I had only lived at Lee Arrendale State Prison for eight weeks before I was called in to see the chaplain. I thought, oh hell no, not again! But in my mind, I was hoping for the best, while preparing for the worst. I knew that someone had died. I just didn't know who it was.

Waiting for two hours outside the chaplain's office, I was on the brink of insanity. I kept praying to God that nothing had happened to any of my children. When the chaplain finally walked in he brought coldness through the door with him. He sat down in his chair, kicked his feet up, and turned over the paper lying face down on his desk.

When the chaplain flipped the paper over in the top right hand corner it read 'name of deceased'. In the space next to it was my grandmother's name, Annie Kate Milling, Shug. If you were waiting to hear that I caused a scene, and acted all dramatic, then you were waiting in vain.

That never happened. I showed absolutely no reaction at all. There were no words or tears. I simply got up out of the seat, walked out of his office, and went back to my cell. I was totally emotionless, and felt completely numb. The loss of my mother had me so traumatized that death itself no longer affected me. Death had lost its sting.

My maternal lifeline was wiped out. My grandmother was my strong point, and we connected after I lost my mother. But now both my mother and grandmother were gone. I knew for sure that I was on my own. My family members didn't invite me to her funeral. That didn't bother me either because I didn't want to go. I was through with death. I swore that the next funeral I would ever attend would be my own. Since I didn't attend my own mother's funeral, I learned that I could live without them.

I sat on my bunk, thinking about my grandmother, but my heart had gone cold. I even tried to make myself cry. Nothing happened. My mind was now focused on my children. My grandmother was dead, and so was theirs. This was the worst nightmare ever. I made myself believe that I was stuck inside of my dreams with no way out. How else could I deal with reality? Well I couldn't, so I created my own. Whenever I crawled out of this hellhole, my life would return to normal.

The following day, I was called to the counselor's office. To my surprise, this visit came with good news. I learned that I finally had a release date with the parole system. My date was set for September 2005. That was only six weeks away. I had no clue as to exactly which day in September, but just knowing that it was September was good enough for me. This had been a long, painful, tiresome journey, and I, without question, was broken. There

was no sense in kicking a dead horse, right? I couldn't be punished anymore for my crimes. I had been punished enough. I had lost some things that would never be returned. I had learned my lesson the hardest way possible.

Those six weeks were the longest of my life. The minutes felt like hours, and the hours crawled along like days. I drew a calendar and hung it on the wall with toothpaste. This was a constant reminder of how many days I had left until I was out of this hole. I had been through, overcome, and survived the worst of it. Everything from here on out would be completely uphill. And I do mean uphill. I could remember sitting and brooding with my thoughts for hours.

Life would actually be harder once I was released. In prison I didn't have my children, and I didn't have any bills to pay. However I was constantly thinking of my children, and how I would be received by them. Would I be welcomed with open arms? Would they resent me?

Emani didn't know her mother at all. She was eighteen months, and had lived her entire life without me. My baby boy, Jayvien, was with his father. It was obvious that my son's father hated me. He had three faces. A Capricorn, he wore grudges like the shirt on his back. Slim could never get pass the day he caught me with Drama. I won't forget it either. That was the day he sent me to exile.

Two months before my mother had passed away, I was surprised when I received court papers in the mail. My son's father had gotten me good. I guess I never suspected he would stoop so low. The abandonment papers were from the magistrate state court of Fulton County. I was the Defendant, and Slim the plaintiff. But wait, that wasn't the shocking part of it all. The shock came when I read the letter that was written by my mother. It stated, *"I can no longer care for my grandson, Jayvien Stanton due to health issues. So I give full care and custody over to his father."* The letter was signed, Joan Milling.

This was devastating because my mother had never discussed this with me. There were other options. She knew my son's father and I had a love hate relationship. Why would she give him my son? Just like some females, he would only use my son as a pawn. I knew that without a doubt!

I remember leaving the mailroom on that fateful day and calling home. My mother, like she always did, accepted the call on the first ring. When I asked her about the letter she was just as surprised as I was! She told me to look at the letter carefully because it wasn't her signature or her handwriting. I examined the letter. Clearly, it was not her writing at all.

So I sent her a copy of all the paperwork and she went to court on my behalf. My mother explained to the judge that the letter was forged. Her actions had prevented me from losing parental rights or custody of Jayvien. The judge ruled that just because I was incarcerated, didn't mean I was an unfit parent.

This fool, Slim, had forged my mother's name, told the court that I abandoned my son, and that they had no clue as to where I was. Not only that, he asked the Judge to grant him sole custody, and to terminate any and

all visitation rights. He knew damn well I was in prison the whole time. The devil is a liar!

But getting back to the story, my other two sons were with my aunt Carrie, my mother's oldest sister. I was just anxious about reuniting with my children, and being a family again. It was on my mind true enough, but I wasn't too concerned about where we would live or how we would survive. I had Phaedra, and the book was already written. I'd done the hard part. All I had to do now was get it typed, and hand it to her. In the meantime, I was sure she would assist me in finding a job. The biggest hurdle now was getting released.

September 1, 2005, was my released date. I knew I was leaving because the night before they had told me to pack up my belongings, and moved me to segregation. The prison officials always sent you to segregation the night before you were to be released to reduce confusion. I couldn't sleep that whole night. I stared through the narrow window in my cell looking up at the stars, and the moon in the sky. My eyes were wide open, searching for my mother the entire night.

"Mommy, I know you are up there somewhere, and I know you have been watching over me. I'm walking out of this prison in the morning a woman, and a mother. I have been blessed with a second chance at life. But this time mom, I'm going to be different. I'm going to turn my negative into positive. I'm going to give back. And I'm going to help heal the world, mom. I promise! I promise you! I promise!" I prayed.

I made a covenant with my mother before I left that prison, and as I walked past those iron gates, I dedicated my life to fulfilling that promise I made to my mother. My brother, Lee waited outside alone in his truck. He had returned to the states for good.

After his basketball contract ended, I don't think he had any desire to ever be that far away from his family again. Neither one of us was there the day our mother died. My brother had to bury our mother on his own. Just like I didn't have him, he didn't have me either. Our entire life, we had been raised close to one another. It was constantly drilled into our heads that we were all each other had in this world.

It felt good to be free! The air was different, and for some reason the sun seemed to shine brighter, but no matter how much I tried to enjoy my freedom I had nothing to be happy about. All that time I spent in prison I survived by making myself believe that my mother, and grandmother were going to be waiting for me. I had not fooled anyone but myself. It was time for me to face reality. I was on my way to pick up my children.

As much as I didn't want to believe it, the truth was that neither my mother nor grandmother was going to be there. I knew that I had to fight this head on. So without any hesitation, I asked my brother to take me to our mother's grave. I needed to come to terms with what was going on. I wanted to get over the devastation of never seeing my mother again. I needed to do this before I came in contact with my children, and that's exactly what I did.

I stood at my mother's graveside with my brother. My mother was

beneath the ground, but we finally had our moment. I saw the headstone with my mother's name on it, and I knew then that it was over. I cried until I made myself sick. My brother carried me from her grave, and drove me around until I could get myself together.

Later that day, we arrived at 306 Ormond St. in Atlanta, Georgia. This was home to me, my mother, my grandmother, and so many other people in the family. Like a dried up desert, my grandmother's home stood, nothing like I remembered. It was clear that my grandmother's presence was obsolete. My grandmother purchased her home in 1955. In the fifty years that she had this home in her possession, none of her utilities were ever disconnected, and she had the same telephone number ever since Bell South was established.

The first thing I noticed was that the lights were disconnected. Then I noticed there was no running water, the phone was off, and the gas had been disconnected as well. The house was filthy and infested with spiders. I looked at my oldest two boys Lekwaun and Leontae. They were very happy to see their mother. I couldn't imagine for the life of me what type of life they had grown accustomed to. Their clothes were three sizes too small, and their shoes were old, beaten up, and dirty. My baby girl, Emani, was running all over the house barefoot. My baby didn't even have a single pair of shoes in her possession. I wasn't angry and I wasn't being ungrateful, I just felt like they deserved more than that.

I was trying my best to make myself comfortable with my present situation. I knew my aunt did the best she could with what she had, but it was just such a cheerlessly, sad homecoming. I tried as hard as I could but I just could not stay in that house. With my grandmother gone, it appeared that all my crack-head cousins had taken over. All types of people were in and out of the house at all hours of the night. Complete strangers stood over me while I slept. I couldn't take it.

There was no way I was going to live there. Not with my children. Everything I looked at, everything I touched, and everything I heard reminded me that my mother and grandmother were gone. This home was not the same place it was before I went to prison. I packed up what little we had, and we left.

My youngest son's father, Slim, suggested that my kids and I live in his house until I got on my feet. That worked for about seven hours. He realized I wasn't interested in having sex with him. I mean for God's sake! I'm sitting here crying. The thought of my mother's death breezed through my mind. I had snot running from my nose, I was screaming at the top of my lungs, and he wanted me to have sex with him. So I packed up my garbage bag full of belongings, took my baby girl, and my three sons. Then we left walking, and ended up at the city shelter.

I had called Phaedra several times. I left her several messages but she never called me back. I should've known something was up when I called her the first day I got out, and received no response, but I continued calling. It was hard for me to imagine that she had just written me off like a bad habit. I myself would lend a hand to a complete and total stranger, so I couldn't

understand what was making her act so cold toward me.

September 3, 2005, I checked into the Atlanta Union Mission homeless shelter. My children and I were residing in one big room along with several other single mothers and their children.

My baby girl cried all night. It wasn't her fault. Emani just didn't know me. She was in an unfamiliar environment and was scared to death. Babies know that they are helpless. They know they can't stop someone from hurting them, just like I couldn't stop the molester from hurting me.

I knew how she felt. The other mothers were becoming frustrated because I couldn't stop her from crying. No matter what I did or which way I moved, my baby was dissatisfied, and didn't mind voicing her opinion. All I could do was sit there hopeless, and miserable. So I cried with her.

When I was released from prison I was given a check for twenty-five dollars, and instructions to report to the parole office in seventy-two hours. You don't leave prison with a job, a home, and a car. Well at least, not everyone does. I know I didn't. All I had was a lot of worries, a bunch of stress, responsibilities, and a criminal record. Once a criminal—always a criminal, You have all heard this statement before, right...? Yeah, well it remained the truth. There was almost no such thing as fully redeeming one's self. Or was there?

It was time for me to report to the parole office. They informed me that I was free to visit the day I left prison, but that turned out to be a lie. Unless of course you maxed out, meaning, you served your total sentence. Even if the justice system did forgive, society never would.

I didn't have anyone to keep my children. I didn't even have enough money to catch the bus to drop them off, and then come back, and pick them up. I couldn't see how that would work. I made a decision that morning, I got my children dressed, I got myself dressed and we waited at the bus stop.

When I walked into the parole office I sat all the way in the back, all the way up against the wall with my children. We sat there as a family side by side. I had to protect my children. Child molesters didn't have a warning sign on their foreheads. We were sitting amongst some of America's worst criminals. I really should have thought twice before I took my children with me, but what other option did I have? If I didn't report they would lock me up, and there was no telling with *whom* my babies would end up going to.

I saw the chief parole officer walk to the front of the waiting room several times looking at me, and discussing my status with one of his peers. After about an hour he called me to the back. My children and I took a seat inside of an office, and he angrily closed the door. He stepped out only to return fifteen minutes later. When he stepped into the office he stared at me, then he stared at my children and said, "Ms. Stanton, don't you know that you are not suppose to bring children to the parole office?"

With the explanation that I was aware of the rule, I told him that I had lost my mother and grandmother to death during my incarceration. I went on to tell him that I was living in a shelter. I had just gotten my children back, and I didn't have anyone to keep them. Every time I thought about my

situation, I instantly felt weak and tears welled up in my eyes. These were the kind of tears that I could not stop from running down my cheeks no matter how hard I tried.

"Ms. Stanton, you need to find someone to keep your children, and report back here in the morning!" He yelled.

I did as he instructed. My aunt kept my children the next morning. I had to take them back to the same home that I vowed never to return to. I suppressed every depressing hair-raising thought to the back of my mind, and began my journey to the parole office.

When I arrived at the parole office I signed my name on the clipboard, and just as soon as I put the pen down, I was immediately escorted to the back. Once I was there, to my surprise, two federal agents were awaiting my arrival to arrest me for conspiracy. They called it conspiracy against the federal government. Before I knew it, I was in the back of their vehicle, handcuffed yet again, and headed to the Richard B. Russell building.

I was in a total state of shock. I was under the presumption that I had served all my time. Now what was going to happen to my children? On the way to the Russell building, I was surprised when federal agent, Steve Lazarus asked me if I was interested in making my case disappear. I was all ears while wondering just exactly how we could make that happen.

The federal agent told me all I had to do was set up Jeezy. I could have literally dropped dead. Not believing what I had just heard. The first thought that came to mind was how the hell did they knew I had any affiliation to Young Jeezy? I hadn't seen or spoken to Jeezy in over two years. So what or who gave the feds the impression that it could be pulled off?

I mean even if I could, Jeezy had nothing to do with my case. Why would I set this man up because I got in trouble on a case that he knew nothing about? Jeezy didn't even know I was in prison.

"How do you know I know Jay?" I asked.

"We have our ways of finding out anything we want to know Ms. Stanton!" He answered with a smug smirk on his face.

He wouldn't admit it, but I already knew. The feds had been listening in on my telephone conversations. When I was locked up, all my phone calls had secretly been recorded. While I was serving time in state prison, the feds had been busy preparing their case against me. Every time I made a phone call they were eavesdropping, listening for any information that might further incriminate me.

Out of curiosity, I played along with their game. I wanted to see what kind of case they were trying to build against Jeezy. Then Agent Lazarus gave it to me straight when he asked, "Do you think you can get him to sell you some drugs?"

In my mind, I was pondering, were they stupid? I'm not a drug dealer. Jeezy knows that! I couldn't believe that they played the game just as dirty as the streets played it. If they wanted Jeezy that bad they would have to get him on their own. I refused to be a part of their ploy. Jeezy had never done

anything to me, or anyone I knew. I was not going to help the feds bring him down. My case was my own responsibility and Young Jeezy had nothing to do with my misdeeds. I couldn't believe what had just happened. I had to get a message back to Jay.

Crying the whole time, I sat in the holding-cell waiting for my turn to see the Judge. When I finally saw the Judge, I begged for mercy. I got down on my knees, and I begged. I asked the Judge why didn't they just come and pick me up directly from prison. Why would anybody allow me to bond with my children, and then snatch me away from them again? I explained what I had been through. There was the loss of my mother and grandmother, and all the time, I kept begging for mercy. And it was nothing more than pure mercy that was granted. The Judge allowed me to sign my own bond. He placed me on the pre-trial release program, and I was once again free. Not only was I now on parole, but I was now on state, county, and federal parole.

Walking away from the Richard Russell building, something triggered in my mind. I wondered if Phaedra Parks already knew what was coming my way. I still hadn't heard from her. What in the world was going on? I had to get in touch with her now. I didn't have anything or anybody. All I kept thinking to myself was when or if this was ever going to be over.

I got on the bus that day and I gazed out the window. The bus passed by the tall glass fixtures that adorned downtown Atlanta. I kept wondering, what next? Phaedra had not returned any of my calls. She was really my only hope. It never once crossed my mind that she had or would even consider turning her back on me.

We had known each other for years. She had bonded not only with me, but also with my children, and my family. I started rationalizing. Maybe she got cold feet. Maybe she thought since my case was being picked up by the feds… I mean I just didn't know. Was there a possibility that she thought I would sing? My mind was drowning in a sea of uncertainty, and I needed life support.

Telling on Phaedra had never once crossed my mind. I had already been dragged through the system. Implicating her now could only make things worse. I thought for sure I would have heard from her by now, so I decided to stop by her office. When I walked up to the receptionist's desk and asked to see her, I saw the green and white striped wall paper which brought back memories.

A phone call was made to her office. The receptionist said, "Ms. Parks, Angela Stanton is here to see you." I was so excited when I learned that she was in the office. I had finally caught up with her. All kind of things began running through my mind as I imagined what our reunion would be like. What would she look like? Would she be happy to see me? What was her excuse for not answering or returning my calls…?

Moments later, the receptionist told me that Ms. Parks was in a meeting, and would be tied up all day. My hopes were dashed and I instantly dropped my head. I didn't want the receptionist to see the despair in my eyes. At this point I was thinking hard and fast. My sixth sense had kicked in

once again, and something just didn't smell right. Before I walked out, I left Phaedra a copy of my manuscript, and the address to the shelter that I was residing at with my children.

Three months passed and still no word from Phaedra. I was at Spondivits, a seafood restaurant on the south side of ATL, hanging with my cousin, Nikki, and enjoying a night out with some old friends. I ran into Jeezy and his entourage. I walked right up to him and said, "Hey Jay baby, how you been? I see you all over the TV doing your thing! I'm so proud of you!" Then I gave him a big hug.

"Girl, I ain't seen you in a long time. Where you been?" he asked.

"I'm doing better now," I said with a smile.

Then I gave him the story about how I had been in prison the last couple of years, and I also told him I needed to talk with him about some business. He gave me a number, I locked it in my phone, and before he left he was sure to extend me an invite to kick it with him and his crew. I politely declined, and I promise that it wasn't because I did not want to go. It was simply that my life was different now. I wasn't the same girl he used to know.

I didn't want to bring up the situation about the feds right then. There were too many people around him, and the atmosphere just wasn't right. I knew there was a certain protocol I had to follow in order to present the information to Jeezy regarding the federal agents. I also knew that he didn't want all of the people around him to be in on his business.

Over the next few days, I called the number several times without ever getting an answer. Finally, after realizing that he had given me his manager's number, Coach K, and not his direct number, I had no other choice but to relay the message to Coach K. Jeezy never called me to inquire, so I figured he had it all worked out.

I had been through the ringer and back trying to get my life back on track, and provide a home for my children. Thirty days was the maximum amount of time I could spend at any shelter. People can't live there forever. Months went by and still no word from Phaedra. By this time I was living in a two bedroom apartment. Small, shaggy, and in the best neighborhood I could afford. I didn't want my sons to grow up around drugs, or exposed to a lifestyle that would land them in prison or the grave.

During those thirty days, I endlessly searched for employment. I was denied job after job after job. I wasn't a dummy. I could read, write, and spell. I mean how difficult could it be to work a job in today's society? It had nothing at all to do with working the job, but rather my criminal past which presented a great barrier. The background check, every time it was done, reminded me that I would never ever be truly free.

Why even release me from prison if it was going to be impossible for me to survive in the free world? As far as I was concerned, I was still in captivity. This method has made the prison system a revolving door and the crime rate will always be on the rise. This was the reason why the number of homeless people increases. This was why there are so many repeat offenders.

You would be set free, but were really not freed! This can prove to be tiring. Do you try figuring it out...? And will that moment come too late?

I applied for Section 8 and Housing Assistance. I was promptly denied by both departments because I was a convicted felon. This latest blow came as a surprise. Anytime I had ever gone to the projects, the place was infested with crime, and convicted felons. I never even wanted to live in the projects, but would have now. It wasn't like we had anywhere else to go.

It got so bad at one point that I auditioned for a job as a stripper. I was hired at a nightclub, and applied for my dancer's permit. It was promptly denied because I was a convicted felon. That also came as a huge surprise to me. It was a major blow to any financial aspirations that I held. You mean to tell me, that because I was a convicted felon, I couldn't stand on a table, and degrade myself for a few lousy dollars? Sh** was getting real serious...

I thought I could bend over and show what I ate for breakfast to anyone I chose. I was just upgraded from modern day slave, so I couldn't get butt-ass-naked? McDonalds wasn't even an option. I didn't have any housing assistance so a two-bedroom apartment was six hundred and seventy-five dollars monthly, and that was in the hood. Of course, the rent didn't include any utilities at all. By the time I worked forty hours at McDonalds earning $5.75 an hour, I still wouldn't have enough money to pay rent. That gig wasn't even worth my time.

The move into a two-bedroom apartment with my children was a start. It was hard, but I began thinking that about a month earlier I was in prison, and I became grateful. Two days before my time expired at the shelter I was downtown job searching and met a man. He was just a friendly guy. We began to talk and I told him my story. For some reason he seemed genuinely concerned. He told me that he had a friend who needed to talk with me, a friend that could possibly help me. The very next evening I met with him and his friend, both angels sent to me from heaven!

The agreement was that I was to marry this man in order for him to stay in the United States. He was from Africa. I would get fifteen thousand dollars just to sign my name on the dotted line. The movie, *Coming to America,* starring Eddie Murphy, started to play in my mind.

Just in case you were wondering, I never even thought twice about it. I agreed without hesitation. The man gave me five thousand dollars cash, and told me he would return to the states in three months with the other ten thousand dollars. We were to be married when he returned. Oddly enough, he never came back. I still have not heard from him or seen him since that day. God works in mysterious ways. He had made a way out when there was no way.

I took the five thousand dollars cash, and got me and my children somewhere decent to live. Then I bought us a ride. A good jump-start to whatever God had in store for us. Once we moved and got settled in our new home, I was able to sit down, and sort through boxes of my belongings which my brother had held in storage for me.

By the time I went through the second box, I found all of the contact

numbers I had on Phaedra. I had her home, office, and cellphone numbers. These were numbers I had forgotten during the eighteen months of my incarceration. I knew I could reach her on her cellphone without a doubt. I grabbed my cellphone and I dialed the number.

"Ms. Parks speaking," she answered on the first ring. The confidence in her tone convinced me that everything would be okay.

"Hey Phaedra..." I responded in a mild mannered voice. "Phaedra, this is Angela. I know you've been busy, but I've been trying to contact you. You know the feds locked me up, right...? I just got out, Phae! I can't leave my kids again! They don't have anyone besides me Phaedra, and you know that! I just don't know what to do!"

I spoke as calmly as I could. I promise you, eyes hadn't seen and ears hadn't heard the words I really wanted to tell her. However, my back was against the wall. I needed her more now than ever. She, on the other hand, acted surprised. It was as if she knew nothing at all about my federal charges. She even seemed shocked, and offended that I had even called her.

When she got over the shock, Phaedra went right into her routine. Pleading her case to the court, she let me know straight up that she was afraid. At least, that's what she told me. Phaedra claimed that her whole life and everything she had worked so hard to build was at stake. I informed her that I had already lost everything, and I had grown tired of hearing about her life. She wasn't even considering my present life situation.

My main concern was, of course, my children. Phaedra told me that she received my manuscript and had passed it along to a friend of hers who was an editor. I didn't know whether to believe this or not. She also told me to inform the court that she would be representing me, and claimed that it would be a year or two before my trial. In the meantime, she wanted to work on getting my manuscript out there.

I could tell by our conversation, or should I say that little thing called discernment, that Phaedra really wasn't feeling me anymore. In my heart, I truly believed that she had decided to cut ties with her criminal side, and live a normal life. That was fine with me, but we had unfinished business. I needed to restore my life, for the sake of my children, and there was no way that I could afford a lawyer to help me beat this case.

Returning to prison meant my children would go to Department of Family and Children Services (DFACS). It was something I refused to let my children experience. If she no longer wanted my friendship, then that was fine, but I needed, and wanted my freedom. My children needed and wanted my freedom. Just like Phaedra had said, it took a year or two before for my trial would begin, so I tried my best to live a normal life, and stay out of the limelight.

The five thousand dollars didn't last forever. Before long, my children were looking to me for shelter, food, and love. I was unable to provide any of the material things, but love came on demand. My mind was going, and I was contemplating putting an end to my existence. Not only did I contemplate suicide, but also taking the lives of my children right along with

mine. This was a thought that I had never shared with anybody until now. It was so hard to love when you are stuck inside of a dark, cold place.

I had grown tired of watching my children suffer, and thoughts of all the tricks I had learned from Phaedra kept breezing through my mind. I had to be strong, so I pushed all thoughts of suicide completely out of my head. I knew I only had one life to live, and I felt that I was sent here for a reason. Lastly, my life wasn't mine to take.

In order to survive, I did what I had to do. I prayed daily that I wouldn't get caught. I know a lot of people don't agree with what was just recorded, but I was not asking you for agreement. I wanted you to understand. If there was no comprehension then try empathizing. In other words, put yourself in my shoes for one second.

Chapter Ten
Three Steps Short Of A Breakthrough

"No weapon that is fashioned against you shall succeed,
and you shall confute every tongue that rises against you in judgment.
This is the heritage of the servants of the Lord and their vindication
from me, declares the Lord."

Isaiah 54:17 (NIV)

I was pumping gas at a service station near my rundown apartment. The kids were in the back seat going crazy. They were fighting, throwing things, and yelling. I guess the normal things that any two, five, eight, and ten year olds did. But on this particular day, it was obviously one of my days when I had put much thought into the reality of my mother no longer being on this earth. I had basically lost it, and right there at the gas pump. I was hysterically crying, I was completely inconsolable.

A kind and understanding gentleman walked up to me. He asked if there is anything he could do to help. At this point, I was behind my car, lying on the ground almost under the tire. I was angrily cursing at the Lord, cursing my life, and cursing my children. Again, I was in a very cold, dark,

and low place.

I spilled my guts out to this total complete stranger. Stumbling through the explanation of how I was on state and federal parole, I told him I was being pressured to find employment, and no one would hire me. I was struggling to provide for my children. My mother had died, and my grandmother died shortly after her. I went on and on spilling my guts while crying my eyes out to this complete stranger. It was as if he was Jesus. Looking back now, I realize that he was another angel God had sent my way.

The very next morning the same complete stranger had given me a job. I began working for the Georgia Department of Transportation (GDOT). I was working as a laborer on the side of highway 285 for two weeks before I brushed shoulders with the manager of human resources, Princess Ferguson. A receptionist position had become available and the company policy was that they offered job placement in house before they advertise with the general public. So without hesitation I applied. Mrs. Ferguson was totally blown away by my ability to dialogue in genuine professional manner. She saw a light shining on the inside of me. It was a light which I thought had been burned out by my past circumstances.

"Thank you for calling the Department of Transportation district seven. Angela Stanton speaking, how may I help you?"

That was my script. I loved my job, and I admired my new boss

Princess. I was very fond of her because when she looked at me she saw no faults in me. She gave me a fair shot and didn't criticize me negatively when I did something wrong. Rather, she would show me the proper way to do it. Princess demanded nothing more than my absolute best. My absolute best was exactly what I provided. This earned me two more promotions in the thirteen months that I worked there.

I had finally found stability. My parole officers and especially my federal pretrial release officer, Lorna Murphy, supported me. She watched me like a hawk to ensure my success. I could tell really, that she truly cared. This was more than just a job for her. I felt she wanted what was best for me and my children. It was a long hard road, but with her encouragement, and her refusal to let me fall, I made it! This went all the way up to my federal trial. Living everyday with uncertainty, not knowing whether or not I would be around to raise my children was a battle in itself.

When my federal trial was set to begin, Phaedra Parks promptly notified the court that she wouldn't be representing me due to a conflict of interest. I had no idea what that meant. I just knew she wasn't coming to court. I didn't have time to try and figure out what was going on with Phaedra. I was at war, fighting for my life.

Federal Judge Linda Evans assigned Susan Hashimi to my case. Ms. Hashimi worked as fast, and as diligently as she could within the time frame she was given. Ms. Hashimi believed in me and believed that I deserved a second chance. I didn't have any doubt in my mind that she wasn't fighting

for me.

My trial began two weeks after I was notified by mail. I made endless trips back and forth to Ms. Hashimi's office. Going over my case from front to back, beginning to end, Ms. Hashimi had given herself a chance to know me as a person, not as a criminal. She even took up donations from her co-workers to help me with the support of my children. Just about everyone in her office donated something, even if it was just one dollar. This helped me tremendously, and my children and I were very grateful. God had placed people in my life who truly wanted to see me succeed.

The morning of my trial, I prayed just as I did every morning. I asked God to have his way. The only way I knew. I had been through enough to realize that man's plans and God's plans were totally different. I was a nervous wreck. Just full of emotions, my mind was racing back and forth.

There was no guarantee that I wouldn't be serving any more time. I was facing five years for conspiracy, and the state time I served had absolutely nothing to do with my federal case. Even though this was all the same crime, Ms. Hashimi had to prove to Federal Judge, Linda Evans that I had learned my lesson, and therefore did not deserve to go back to prison.

I sat on the right side of Judge Evans with my attorney. Everett Tripodis sat on the left side of Judge Evans with his attorney. Ms. Hashimi and I sat silently, and listened as Everett's Lawyer pleaded his case for him. We listened as his attorney told Judge Evans that I was the mastermind behind the whole operation, and that he worked for me under my direction.

That was a good one! Now it started making sense to me where the investigators got all of their information. Ms. Hashimi was quick to object. She stated that I didn't have any related crimes in my criminal background, but Everett Tripodis and his brother Apollo Nida on the other hand were both on federal parole for the same exact crimes at the time of their arrest.

Judge Evans held a stare that could pierce any soul. She was an honest and fair Judge who made sure that she read between each and every line. Judge Evans did not believe I was the mastermind. She was concerned with how much involvement I actually had in this Federal racketeering scheme.

Before Judge Evans sentenced Everett she gave him the opportunity to speak for himself. He stood before the court and begged the Judge for his release. His excuse was because his mother was sick, and he wanted to be by her side before she passed away. I could have vomited all over the courtroom at that point. I was noticeably sick to my stomach.

Judge Evans was reasonable, but firm. She sentenced Everett Tripodis to five years right in front of me. He was escorted out of the courtroom and I was next. I could hear my mother's words again.

"Girl one day your mouth is going to get you in a world of trouble!"

I thought about her words because they were true. I was going back to prison and there wasn't any doubt in my mind. My legs were shaking uncontrollably. My bowels were weak. I was having hot flashes, and I just knew it was over for me. The thought of my children suffering anymore than they already did took the life right out of me.

My federal parole officer, Lorna Murphy, stood before the court, and she testified on my behalf. Something she told me that she'd never done for any parolee throughout the duration of her career.

Lorna Murphy spoke about the changes she observed in me, and about how I had transformed from nothing into something. I was a success story. She shared the reports she had received from my counselor, and the reports from the clinical psychologist. They all attested to the fact that I had been completely rehabilitated.

My brother testified on my behalf, and Ms. Hashimi proved my case. She provided the court with a letter from the Georgia Department of Transportation stating that I was an excellent employee, and that I had a great future with the company. Ms. Hashimi showed the court that I was an asset, and not a liability. I had become a law abiding, taxpaying citizen. Sending me back to prison would be a waste of taxpayer's money, and would definitely serve as an injustice to my children.

When it was it was my turn to stand before the court, and plead my case. I stood and focused on the judge then said, "First and foremost I want to apologize to you Judge Evans and to the court as well. I take full responsibility for all my actions Judge Evans. And I want to just throw myself upon the mercy of the court. I heard Everett Tripodis say that he wanted to be by his mother's side before she passes. Well Judge Evans, my mother did pass during my incarceration as did my grandmother, and due to certain circumstances I wasn't at either funeral. I also gave birth to my daughter handcuffed to a bed, and I wasn't able to be a mother to her until she was eighteen months old. Those things I would like the court to take into consideration before my sentencing. Those things are far worse than any prison sentence. I would have rather served twenty years, and come home to my mother than serve the eighteen months I served that took away everything I have ever cherished! Thank you your honor for taking the time to hear my words."

Judge Evans stared at me long and hard before she made her decision. Every time she opened her mouth to say something, she looked directly at me, shook her head, and sat back in her chair. I knew that she was thinking intensely. But what killed me was that I had no idea what it was that she was thinking. The courtroom was quiet enough to hear a pin drop. The anticipation of what her words would be had the entire courtroom on edge.

I was silently praying while awaiting the verdict. My fate was hanging in the balance. Through the corner of my eyes, I could see my brother, head bowed and praying. Lorna Murphy was doing likewise, even Ms. Hashimi was praying on my behalf. I felt my mother's presence in the courtroom with me. I knew this in my heart, even though I couldn't see her, I couldn't hear her, but I could definitely feel her.

We were all on the same accord that day, asking God for the same blessing, and God answered our prayers. Judge Evans sentenced me to three years supervised release. It meant that I would not have to go back on the inside. I could indeed stay on the outside with my children, but I would be on parole for the next three years.

I must have cried, and thanked God all day. It was such a lovely day! He had delivered me from the snares of the devil once again. My life almost began to feel normal. My trial was behind me, and I didn't have any pending charges. Shaheed was long gone out of my life. He had been sentenced to life on his murder charge. I had a career ladder job with benefits, my children were in counseling. We had our own apartment, and our own ride. I was so happy. God had finally restored my life. Thank you sweet JESUS!

Over the course of the next few months, my life was pretty average. I went to work then returned home, cooked, ironed, washed clothes, and cared for my children. I worked extra hard to try and build our relationship again.

I was a normal law-abiding citizen. I went from being a hot girl who was worried about the law, to having a job, and being a full-time mother. No more running the streets with my cousins. No more side hustles. I wasn't living from check to check, but it sure felt like it because there was never any money left to save. Every time I paid all the bills, the kids needed something else. If it wasn't clothes it was shoes, if it wasn't shoes it was food or gas for the car. There was always something to eat up whatever spare change I may have had lying around.

By this time, I had endured so much in life that the negative came right along with the positive. In other words, I hoped for the best, but prepared for the worst. I learned to take the good with the bad. So it would pretty much take a lot to get me upset, or out of character. I kept striving to be the best I could be on my job. And with every free moment, I tried to make up for lost time with my children.

My highest position with the Georgia Department of Transportation was in the personnel department. I had been promoted yet again. I was now the person that sat behind the desk during the interview process.

When I interviewed people I always looked for sincerity. If they were sincere, honest, and up front about their past, I figured they deserved a chance. There were people just like myself who already had strikes against them, and would work ten times harder. They were driven harder by some unknown force because they knew they had everything to lose.

My coworkers were astonished by my growth in the company. They witnessed my hunger, and my eagerness to survive. One glance at me and all they saw was an outer shell. They had no idea what was deep down inside of me. They didn't know that my job was all my children and I had.

One of my coworkers applied for the position I had just been granted. Not only did she apply for it, she had basically already claimed it. She was sadly disappointed, and she strongly disagreed with the decision to give me the position. But hey, may the best woman win. And hands down I was the best! I was the best because I had to be.

What choice did I have with so many strikes against me? This job was the best thing I had going, and I was going to hold on to it for dear life. I knew this particular coworker had it in for me. I saw her dirty looks, and her snares toward me were obvious. But not only just that, I even dreamed of

her in my home one night. In the dream she was chasing me in my hallway. She was the size of a T- Rex. She was angry, starving, and hunting me down, making me her prey. That sounds crazy, but let me get to the next part.

It was Mother's Day, and I was on my way to work, listening to the Yolanda Adams morning show. I loved Yolanda Adams. Her lyrics had been inspirational to me. When my mother passed during my imprisonment, one of my fellow slave mates gave me a CD player and a copy of Yolanda Adams' latest album, 'The battle is not yours'. God knows, that song had saved my life. Her voice and her words restored my soul. If I ever get to meet her one day, I will be sure to tell her how much her lyrics meant to me. But nonetheless, everyone was calling in giving thanks for their mother, and I was obviously not only moved by the outpouring of affection, but also by the love shown on this particular Mother's Day.

I felt the urge to call-in and share my pain with the world. It would be my way of letting the world know that people should never take their mothers for granted. So I did! I shared my story about how my mother died while I was in prison, and how I wish I had done things differently.

When I got to work that morning, my coworker, the one I dreamed of, had heard me on the radio. So she asked, "Angela were you on the radio this morning?"

I said, "No." Then I walked right by her desk.

"That's funny. I could've sworn that was your voice I heard. It was someone that sounded just like you though!" She said. I left it at that and never responded.

A couple of days later, I arrived to work. And about five minutes after my arrival, my boss called me in her office. She informed me that I was being terminated and that there was absolutely nothing she could do about it.

Apparently, someone had gone online, pulled up my criminal background, and sent an anonymous letter to the commissioner of GDOT. The letter stated that I had been in prison for forgery, and that I should not be allowed to work in the personnel department with access to everyone's personal information.

The commissioner made the decision herself to fire me. There was nothing my boss or her boss could do about it. There it was; the enemy had won again. The devil hated when I shared my story with people. My story held the power to heal.

I called the commissioner and I begged her to at least demote me or transfer me to another unit. I begged, "Please ma'am... I'm a single mother. I have no other way to provide for my children!"

I told her everything I could to keep my job, but she had no emotion. She truly could have cared less just like the counselors my mother sent me to talk to after I died at the age of five. Like getting rid of a dirty rag, she threw away my life, and my children's well-being went with it.

A few months after I was fired, she made the national headlines herself. The commissioner of the GDOT was caught in a scandal. But unlike

me, she was afforded mercy. How ironic? When she cried about how she was a single mother of one, she got to keep her job. I'll just be damned!

I started to go pay her a 'remember me' visit. I wanted to make her remember my situation during her time of discomfort. Just to see if she could empathize with me. I mean, seeing how she had no sympathy for me back then. Maybe she would be more understanding. Well, we all know that God doesn't like ugly! No... Not one bit.

Nevertheless, I was back to square one. Now what? I cried when I lost my job, of course. That was simply because I didn't see any other way out at that time. But after time passed, I realized that my job with GDOT was just a bridge. It was just a bridge to carry me from the beginning, to my federal trial, to now. Without my job with the GDOT, Judge Evans would have most certainly sent me back to prison. My job showed that I was being productive. It was a reason for me not to commit crimes. No sense crying over spilled milk. God was in control now. Before long the bills were piling up again. The rent was due, and my children were begging for everything they saw on television.

I needed to talk to someone. On the verge of having a nervous break-down, I made an appointment to see my OB/GYN doctor. Dr. Neal Freeman had proved to be a special person in my life. He worked at the neighborhood welfare clinic, Southside Health Care. His office was walking distance from my grandmother's home. Dr. Freeman had provided all of my prenatal care for my three sons. He even delivered two of them.

Every time I went to Dr. Freeman's office it was like going to see my father. He gave me endless countless sessions on what I should be doing to get my life together. Being my doctor for over thirteen years, he knew my story all too well. I was four months pregnant with Emani the last time Dr. Freeman saw me. He wondered why I had just dropped off of the face of the earth.

On this particular visit, I couldn't hold my composure. I wasn't sure if I was going to make it after the latest blow life had given me. I told Dr. Freeman about my journey to prison, my release, my job, and how I was back to nothing. I had my recently finished manuscript with me. It was my life and everywhere I went, I carried it along with me. I showed it to him, and briefly detailed what it was about.

After intently listening, the look in his eyes beneath his square framed glasses, said it all. Dr. Freeman is a tall bright-skinned, handsome man. He was amazed and immediately started telling me about his friend Goldie Taylor, and about all of her accomplishments. Goldie Taylor was a famous television personality with connections in the literary field. Her biggest achievement of all to me was the fact that she was a successful author. That was my dream.

Dr. Freeman gave me his word that she would help me. Before I left his office that day I had Goldie Taylor's personal number in hand. It was the blessing I had been waiting for. This provided me with the incentive I needed to keep on pushing. Before calling Goldie, I went to the public library, and

did some research into her life. I will be the first to say that I was blown away by what she had accomplished.

The day that I spoke with Goldie, I could tell that there was something in her voice which let me know that everything would be alright. She was all ears when I shared my story. I told her about the sexual abuse I endured as a child. I was surprised by the fact that she told me that she had also been a victim. There was an instant bond welding between us. I asked her if she knew Phaedra Parks. She told me that she did, but I didn't go into any details at that point because Goldie and I still needed to feel each other out. She agreed to meet with me the next week. I sent her my manuscript by email so she could read it in the meantime.

The following week I met Goldie Taylor in the lobby of the Ritz-Carlton hotel on Peachtree St. She came with gifts in hand. Goldie was a short woman compared to me. She had hair the color of gold, golden skin, and golden eyes. I could easily see why her name was Goldie. She had given me a signed copy of her own book, several other books and a gift card from Barnes and Noble. In addition to that, she had a contract for me to sign. She was so moved by my story, not only my story, but the stories that resided within the pages of my first book, 'Life Beyond These Walls'.

She agreed to represent me as my agent. Many promises were made, and I was left with a new outlook on life. With my contract signed and dated the next few weeks, I seemed to be making progress. Goldie had already explained to me the grueling process of editing, so I wasn't too pressed about how quickly this project would jump. I was just happy the process had started.

My life was beginning to take a perfect shape. I had stopped stressing, and was now dreaming of all the things I would be able to provide for my children. Then on a day when I was feeling good, there came the one phone call that shifted my life yet again. The phone rang, and looking at the caller ID, I saw that it was Goldie Taylor calling. Feeling the excitement building inside me, I immediately grabbed the phone. My smile quickly turned to a frown. Goldie bluntly and unremorsefully explained that she had received a contract from Warner Books. It was one that she had been waiting on. The contract clearly stated that she could not work on any other projects. Just like that, my dream had died a quick death. It was the last telephone call I ever received from Goldie Taylor. I was hurt because she dropped me like a hot rock, but at the same time I was genuinely happy for her success. I wasn't going to hate on her for being something I wasn't. Oh well, back to square one. Back to absolutely nothing!

I hated taking the position that I took, but it is what it is! You can't live without money, not in this world. Not in anybody's world. I had to do what I had to do to take care of my children. I was back in the streets, doing what I do best. This included whatever it took to make a way for me and my children, I did it.

Always smart though, I knew I had to have a legal gig going on. I had a hidden talent that hadn't been exposed to the world yet. I was a poet, and street poetry was my calling. I was always known for rapping. I knew

people in the music industry, and those contacts came from me dating Drama.

I had been in the studio with a lot of Atlanta rappers before they made it big. My love for rhymes allowed me to cross paths with many of today's famous artist including Young Dro, Shawty Lo, Fabo, Big Kuntry Kane, TI, Gucci Mane, DJ Jelly and a host of others.

The first time I really made any noise was when I remixed Shawty Lo's single, "Dope boys got these girls gone wild," I switched it to, "Dope girls got these boys going wild," I went to his studio, got with his producer, Born Immaculate, and remixed his song, on his set.

Now that was how one makes a huge statement! It was funny watching all his boys coming to the back of the studio, standing around the booth, and staring at me through the glass. They needed to witness my act with their own eyes. They couldn't believe what they were hearing. I was the truth. Believe that!

I stayed in the studio, destined to make a hit. Something had to give. The book I wrote in prison was on hold because I didn't know what to do with it. Phaedra was acting brand new, I guess she had cut us all off, and gone on with her life. I wasn't tripping too hard though. I was really just glad that all of it was over. I never truly understood why she refused to help me rebuild my life. I mean, she was all for it when we were doing illegal stuff. I had one major thing on my side. I had a book now, a book that every young girl in the world needed to read.

Why wouldn't she be all for it when it was something legal and positive? If our relationship had been restricted to boss and worker then I would have had a better understanding. But Phaedra was my friend. She was a godmother to my son Jayvien. She didn't even give me the honor of sitting down with me to describe my mother's last day on earth. What had I done to push her so far away? I just couldn't understand it.

Recording a hit was now at the top of my to-do list. This was prior to Nicki Minaj hitting the music scene. There weren't any new female rappers out, so the market was wide open. There had to be a way out for my children and me. I was good at anything I put my mind to, so I knew it was the perfect time to come out with a hit. I was sitting at my son's father's house. When I heard Decatur Slim singing a hook.

"Get a life, get some swag... Stop popping at the mouth, and pop tags..."

The hook kept going off in my head. Like every five minutes, I would hear it again. After a while, the light bulb went on inside my head. That was it. This was going to be the hook for my hit song!

I sat down with my son's father and my cousin, Scott, not just by chance, but because they were experienced. Scott had already recorded and released an album, and Decatur Slim was one of the best rappers I had ever come across. We wrote the song in less than an hour and we knew it was a hit. We went straight to Patchwerk Recording Studios and recorded it. 'BOY STOP' by Lady Lenox.

The song was hot! Knowing a hit when he heard it, the producer at

Patchwerk jumped right on it. He took me straight to Hitt Afta Hitt Entertainment to meet with Johnnie Cabbell. Johnnie heard the song and was digging it. At first, he tried me. It was to be expected. He asked me if I wanted to sell my song to Mac Breeze, a local female rapper he managed. She had made her claim to fame when she was featured on Gucci Mane's single, 'Go Head'.

Yes, I did say try me! That song was made for me. No flexing, no lying, just the honest truth, and you had to have lived that life in order to rap that song. I explained it to Johnnie just like that! Straight up! He told me that he had to go out of town, and wanted to meet with me in two weeks when he returned.

During those two weeks the song started playing everywhere in Atlanta, on the radio, in the nightclubs, and in all the strip clubs. People were feeling that song everywhere. Straight up! My brother Lee, my cousins and friends were calling saying they were somewhere, and heard it being played. That was one of the best feelings in the world. Johnnie Cabbell had managed just about every hot rapper in the south from Shawty Lo to Gucci Mane. If you wanted to get in the game and you lived in the city, Johnnie was the man you needed on your team.

I spoke with Johnnie several times while he was out of town. I shared my struggle with him. After hearing my story, he told me that the path of crime my life had taken, my struggle, and the force that was driving me reminded him of Shawty Lo. I talked to him about the book I'd written in prison, 'Life beyond these walls', and my plans.

The plan I had was to release 'Boy Stop' as a single just to get the attention of the youth, and make a name for myself. Once I accomplished that, I wanted to push the book, right along with launching a national campaign for my nonprofit organization 'Don't Ask, Just Tell and Stop the Silence'. I formed this not for profit agency to help worldwide victims of sexual abuse. That was my dream. I thought it was a good idea and so did he. I honestly believed he saw my vision for helping others.

Spring of 2008, Memorial Day was around the corner, and everybody I was affiliated with was going to Miami. So I went also. My whole purpose for going was to promote the song. But I hadn't been anywhere since returning from prison. My children were with my younger cousin, Monique. She agreed to stay over at my house and keep them.

I kept thinking that a little vacation wouldn't hurt. I called up my homeboy, Jay at Patchwerk and had five thousand CD's printed. Me, my partner, Renita, and another one of our home girls rented a vehicle and headed for Miami. We didn't even have a hotel room. We just made up our mind to go and left.

Everybody and they mama was in Miami. South Beach was rocking off the chain. Parties were everywhere. Thousands of people, all the rappers, and all of the entertainers were living it up. Jeezy was there, riding around in his blue Lamborghini. I wanted to give him a copy of my CD. I spoke to him, he hollered back. I started to approach him just to give him a copy of my CD. He had a look in his eyes which told me he didn't want to be bothered, so I

turned, and walked away. I wasn't about to sweat him. I knew him too well when he was Jay. I wasn't stuck on the Young Jeezy hype.

Renita got the DJ to play 'Boy Stop' while thousands of people were on the beach. She was a genius. The crowd loved it! Shawty Lo was hot at this time. He was on the beach and he heard it too. It felt so good to look at thousands of people listening to my words. They were all jamming to the sound of my voice. About an hour later, in the lobby of the Sagamore Hotel, I saw Shawty Lo and he commended me on the song. He told me that he definitely wanted to do a remix when we got back to Atlanta. I was ecstatic! He told me to call Johnnie Tuesday and make an appointment for the studio.

That was all I needed to hear. It felt like Christmas. I called my cousins back home, and told them to start celebrating. Everybody was so excited about the news that they just wanted to know when I was coming back to Atlanta.

"Sunday…!" I screamed with excitement. From that point on, I started to enjoy the rest of my vacation.

I had something to look forward to when I got back home. I emailed Phaedra an mp3 copy of my song. Everybody knew it was a hit. Since she had connections with all the record companies, I thought she would at least put it out there for me. But I never heard back from her. I wasn't about to let that stop me. I was disgruntled a lot by this. I mean it wasn't like I was asking her for handouts. I was creating opportunities for her to make money as well. I was now really tripping off Phaedra's ability to distance herself from me. She always pointed out that we were family.

When I made it back to Atlanta, I felt one hundred pounds lighter, and I was relieved that something had finally worked out in my favor. This was the closest I had ever come to living my dream. As per my conversation with Shawty Lo, I called Johnnie on Tuesday. He was still out of town, and promised to call me when he returned. I was on pins and needles, anxious and ambitious. I was even counting the money I hadn't made yet, and about to burst with excitement. Afraid that I would miss his call, I checked my phone every fifteen minutes.

Two days later, Johnnie called to tell me that he had just landed at Hartsfield Airport. He offered to pay me for a ride. Johnnie told me that his cars were parked at his home. I understood. I would not want to leave my fancy, high priced car at anyone's airport either. My stomach was cramping due to my menstruation, it had been cramping all night, but I was only about five minutes away from the airport. I needed the money, and I wanted to discuss the remix anyway. Doing the remix with Shawty Lo had been the only thing on my mind. I could barely sleep.

Johnnie was already waiting outside when I arrived at Hartsfield airport. I spoke to him on the phone as I pulled in. By the time he had his seatbelt on, he was already deep in conversation with someone else, and all of his conversation was strictly business. I listened closely while playing it off, as if I wasn't interested. But I heard the deals he had sealed for Shawty Lo, and I was impressed with his ability to make things happen. He lived about twenty

minutes from the airport, right off Moreland Avenue behind Club Blaze.

As I rode with this man who I had no reason not to trust, I never perceived him to be any threat to my well-being. He invited me inside his home. His mother greeted me at the door, and that only made me feel more secure. I felt that I had sealed the deal with Johnnie. Why else would he take a stranger to his home? He escorted me upstairs to his living quarters where he had his master bedroom, and a brown plush leather sofa in the far right of the room. I took my seat on his sofa and watched him stretch out across his beautifully adorned California King bed. Johnnie was dressed in Gucci from head to toe.

I sat there about another thirty minutes and listened as he continued to book shows back to back. His mother yelled upstairs that she was stepping out for a moment. A few minutes later, he hung up his phone, and asked me to give him a massage. I should have known then that something wasn't right. But like a dummy, I fell into the trap. I began massaging his shoulders. Mind you, he was fully dressed, and so was I.

The next thing I knew I was thrown down on the bed like yesterday's laundry. Johnnie used the upper part of his body to pin me down on the bed, restraining me and preventing any movement. Johnnie was six feet tall and weighed nearly three hundred pounds. I couldn't believe what was happening. I was being raped. I cried out to Johnnie, begging him to stop.

"Johnnie what are you doing? I'm on my period! Give me a couple of days, and I'll come back!" I pleaded with him, but nothing worked. It was as if he had been possessed by something. His outer appearance changed. I felt absolutely helpless.

Johnnie ripped off my jeans like they were a piece of paper. Then he stuck his finger inside of me, and yanked out my tampon. I thought for sure after seeing the bloody tampon he would've stopped. But he didn't. He never thought to use a condom. He rammed himself inside of my bloody vagina while ignoring my pleas for him to stop. Biting me and pinning me down seemed to excite him only more. The more I hollered and screamed, the harder he pushed himself inside me.

I was afraid. I had no clue if my life was going to end that day. I didn't know what was going to happen next when he got through handling his business. I couldn't understand why he was doing this to me. This was Johnnie. He had money, and he could have had any girl in the city. What the f**k...?

Being molested when you were a young helpless child, and being raped when you became a grown woman were two totally different things. There were two totally different effects on my mind and body. I was all grown up, I had paid my dues, and I didn't have to answer to anyone. I worked or hustled for everything I had. I hadn't asked anyone for spit. What gave Johnnie the right to take something from me?

When Johnnie got through, to my surprise, he rolled over and fell right asleep. I sat there for a moment. Astonished! I snapped back rather quickly, and grabbed my jeans. I left him lying there in the bed. I got in my car, and drove to the nearest gas station and called Phaedra. She answered on

the first ring. This was only because I had changed my phone number since the last time we talked. She probably thought I was one of her clients. I was crying hysterically when I told her what happened. Phaedra knew Johnnie, and it sounded as if she was trying her best to comprehend what I had just told her. I asked, *"Phaedra, what do I do?"*

"If he obviously raped you, well call the police!" She said. My mind started to spin. *"Call me after you speak with the authorities,"* she said.

I hung up from Phaedra then I called the DeKalb County Police. The police responded within minutes. I was immediately taken to a hospital for a rape kit. Johnnie was woken up by the crime scene investigation unit (CSI). He hadn't even bathed and was still lying in bed with the bloody tampon. Now that was just nasty.

Of course, he told the police that the sex was consensual. The detective already told me that he was going to do that. My biggest worry now was what type of disease he had given me. He didn't even know me like that. He had only seen me twice before the rape occurred.

What type of man had forced-sex with any female, especially one they don't know, and while she was on her period? That thought alone had me going insane. To me, he had nothing to lose by his actions. Johnnie was charged with strong-arm rape. The next couple of days were absolutely crazy.

The first telephone call I received was from Shawty Lo. I know Johnnie had him call me, but what Johnnie didn't know was that I already knew Lo. I use to date a friend of his that went by the name, Po Slim. Even though Slim and I were no longer together, he still wanted to see me succeed.

It was funny how I had first met Slim. I was walking through the mall in the West End. It was about a year after my release. Summer of 2006, he noticed me walking in the mall. He had an appetite for tall women. Slim was very persistent. He kicked it and I had no problem speaking to him.

We walked together and we talked about my struggle. And to say the very least, he was amazed by my hunger. Tied to the streets himself, he did not appreciate crimes committed against women and children. Shawty Lo knew what the deal was, but he was stuck in the middle, trying to patch things up. True enough, Johnnie was dead-ass wrong.

However, there was a conflict of interest. Johnnie had Lo's career in the palm of his hands. If Johnnie went to jail that meant everybody associated with him would lose. I felt some sort of compassion toward this. I had a similar story with Phaedra and I knew where he was coming from. Lo begged for Johnnie's life and was willing to agree to whatever demands I had if I would drop all charges. Shawty Lo made the first offer.

Okay now things were getting difficult. The next call came from Fabo, I already knew him too before D4L, back when he was down with Raheem the Dream. They were talking numbers, *big* numbers for my silence. The first song I ever made was with Fabo. He was my partner. He said, "You got your man!" Basically letting me know that whatever I wanted Johnnie would adhere to. He also didn't hesitate to inform me of my risk of becoming a target. On another note my rap career was in the palm of my hands. It was

strictly up to me. I thought about Fabo's words. True enough, but Fabo didn't know about my past. I knew that I would be receiving another call, so I went to Wal-Mart, and purchased a mini-tape recorder.

Moments after I opened the recorder, and figured out how to work it, the phone rang. The Caller ID read, Johnnie 'Hitt AftA Hitt.' I pressed record and let the phone ring a couple more times before answering the call. I was trying to get my thoughts together. Then the call dropped before I had a chance to answer it. I pressed record again before dialing the number back.

Johnnie signed his life away during this taped telephone conversation. He apologized for raping me. He admitted to removing my tampon, but didn't look at it because he didn't want to see the blood. He told me he couldn't help himself because I was red with tattoos and he has a thing for girls like that. Johnnie agreed to give me money, put me on his payroll, and push my career. Keep in mind this was all recorded. I still have the tape in my possession. I listen to it every time I want to be reminded of the enemy, and how he comes to kill, steal, and destroy.

After the conversation with Johnnie, I played the tape back to make sure I had it recorded, and I did. This was evidence I would need to prove that I wasn't lying. The evidence I needed to prove that I wasn't just another groupie trying to get money out of a celebrity. I called Phaedra to let her know that I had the tape, and that they were offering me money. I needed her guidance because I didn't know what to do or how to handle this situation. Phaedra never returned any of my calls.

I told the detective about the tape, and he asked me to bring it in. I also told him about the offers that were presented to me. He told me that that was the way these things go because these guys have money. They don't understand the word 'NO' and they pay their way out of everything. This was not what I had planned. I was supposed to meet Johnnie, get a date for the studio, and remix my song. How did things go south? I mean what happened?

All hell broke loose when my brother, Lee, found out. He was dealing with a lot around this time. The death of our mother was still fresh. Everyday felt like she had just died the day before. Lee's wife suddenly became ill. She was diagnosed with cancer. Then his only sibling and baby sister had been raped by Johnnie.

What Johnnie did was the straw that broke the camel's back. I tried consoling Lee all I could, but he was inconsolable.

"This f#@%-pu**y-a**-ni**a raped my sister? My Sister! Oh I'm finna kill this bi**h-a** ni**a!" Lee shouted.

Tears of anger streamed down his face. Lee held his 45 semi automatic in his hand. He carefully loaded each bullet. I stared in awe because I'd never seen my brother like this before. Mother always said, "The difference between my two children is night and day."

Lee was always quiet, humble, and mild mannered. I, on the other hand, seven years younger and always ready to get it poppin'. I mean I was

rowdy. At that dreadful moment, it seemed as if my brother and I switched places. He was just as determined to kill Johnny as I was to kill Curtis. The police were already involved.

I told Lee that if he killed this man then he would be the first suspect. My brother rose up like a giant and roared.

"SO...? I DON'T GIVE A F#@%! I'M A MAN! I'M NOT A F#@%ING C-O-W-A-R-D!" My enraged brother shouted.

Then he sprinted toward the door. In my mind I already knew where he was headed. Lee and I were very close. I had told him everything. He knew where Johnnie lived, and he knew exactly where Johnnie's office was on Peachtree Street in downtown Atlanta. Diving across the living room floor, I wrapped both arms around his legs, tackling him. Then I begged him not to throw his life away. I told him to think of my niece, Mya, his only daughter.

"If you go to prison, who's gonna be here to protect her?" I asked.

Finally my words grabbed him, and he heeded. He stopped. This giant of a man fell to the floor, and cried like a baby. I held him in my embrace. I was the closest touch he had to our mother. Together we cried and I promised that it would be okay. Just like our mother always told us, "There's more than one way to skin a cat."

Looking back to that day, I still can't for the life of me understand what Johnnie was thinking. My best guess, he assumed I needed him more than he needed me. He knew my story all too well, knew I didn't have many choices in life. I guess he thought that he could just rape me. Then I would just let it go because I needed him on my team.

But I wasn't going for that. I couldn't. I didn't have any say so about what happened to me when I was five, but I was in control this time. Whether Johnnie understood it or not this was very personal for me, and he was in violation. I wasn't about to let this ride. No! F#@% that!

I was worried about a lot of things. I thought about the conversation I had with Fabo, and becoming a target. Remember, I'm from the streets and I know how people get down. Johnnie had a lot of young guys on his team basically sweating him or riding his coattail. They all wanted to make it. Rap was a way out of the hood for many people who had no other way out. Johnnie could make that happen for them, and I was sure that in return for that favor they wouldn't have a problem with getting rid of me.

The police weren't willing to provide me any protection. My children and I didn't have anything or anywhere to go. I started weighing my options, again looking at my children. I wanted to do what was best for them. Thirty thousand dollars seemed like a lot at the time, and it would be enough to drastically change me and my children's lives.

He had agreed to push my song, and make me the next hot artist, but I had already made up my mind. I didn't want to work with Johnnie. I never even wanted to see him again. There was no way I was going to walk around everyday like nothing happened. I had to do that my entire life. Every family reunion, and graduation, I was good on that part of the game. I didn't care

who he was, and much less for what he had. I was sure I could have gotten more money from Johnnie in a civil suit after a criminal investigation, but the risk of becoming a target was too great.

Not only was I a target, but Johnnie's attorney had already threatened to have my parole violated for extortion if they ever heard anything about the rape again. This was another reason I had needed Phaedra's guidance, but she had completely rid herself of me. Her lifestyle had changed from the old days of being a crook. She just refused to help me. She gave me all the direction in the world when we had illegal dealings, but the rules of the game had changed. I wasn't privy to the rule book anymore. So I did what I had to do. What I thought was best for my children and myself, I went with that. I met Johnnie at the Fulton County Library, signed an agreement not to prosecute, and took the money.

I used that money to make moves. After relocating my family to another home, I purchased a new vehicle, took my babies to the beach in Florida, and I also published my first book, 'Life Beyond These Walls', which I had written while I was in prison.

Dr. Alveda King, a prolife activist, was instrumental in providing me with some much necessary help along the way. I had pretty much given up on my rap career after that incident. I was too apprehensive and didn't want to do music anymore. Johnnie not only raped me, but he had also snatched my dream away from me.

The only thing I wanted to do now was share my story with young women. I had experienced and survived just about every hurt known to the human being. I got on the telephone that day and called all over the city until I found a program for young women that would give me an opportunity to volunteer my services.

When I first met Dr. Alveda King, the niece of slain civil rights leader, Dr. Martin Luther King Jr., she was counseling at a pregnancy crisis center for teen girls. I shared my life story with her, and she was completely blown away.

Dr. King's mission is to fight everyday for the lives of children. She looked at me as child, a child that needed to be born again. She promised me the first day I met her that she was going to help me get my life on track, and she did. She immediately began my healing process by allowing me to help the young women in her center. I never knew that my life story could prove to be so rewarding. The day I visited with Dr. King in her office, changed the focus of my whole existence.

Chapter Eleven
Ultimate Betrayal

*"Anyone who withholds kindness from a friend forsakes
the fear of the Almighty."*

Job 6:14(NIV)

Prior to this book, and over the last few years, my life had been a constant struggle. Becoming one with me, myself, while forgiving I, proved to be a much harder task than I thought it would ever be. The process of reconciliation wore on me, and it almost took me out. Trying to suppress all of my bad memories was actually harder than remembering them. Dr. King kept her promise. She remained very active in my life. Helping me see past the pain, Dr. King gave me a newfound love for the misguided and mistreated children throughout the world. She singlehandedly guided me to a safer place.

My first book signing for the book, 'Life Beyond These Walls', was at the Martin Luther King center in Atlanta, GA. I chose that title because I knew that you could be locked behind mental walls in your mind, not just

walls made of concrete. I felt so honored. Dr. King made one call and it was done. She put me on a pedestal. She showed me that I had worth.

Ms. Lorna Murphy showed up in addition to other parole officers I had over the course of my three years, Tammy Boone and Amy Roberts. My old boss from GDOT, Princess showed up and her boss, Rachel Brown, did as well. All of these people came out, and they showed their support. My cousin, Angie, and other people who not only believed in me, but knew I deserved a second chance, came out. I could never thank them enough. These were the people who truly helped me. Their belief in me along with my faith equaled success.

Of course Phaedra never showed her face. I was disappointed, but not at all surprised. In fact, the last time I spoke with Phaedra was when Johnny raped me in June of 2008. I often wondered about Phaedra, and how her life turned out. Every time that I would think of her, my brain would quickly remind me that she had gone on with her life. And I had to do the same thing. Phaedra wanted to leave the dirty deeds of our past in the past. That was understandable to me. I wouldn't wish what I'd been through on my worst enemy.

Sharing my story as a preventative method to keep young women from making the same mistakes was a proven success. It took me almost thirty-two years to realize that I was not a mistake, and that my life had true meaning. It had value. After almost thirty-two years, I found my purpose. There were countless counseling sessions, and being taught to think after the thought, I finally found peace within. I was now able to live my life as a normal adult. I was finally able to love my children, love my life, and not resent anything at all about life. Ever! This was my life now. I felt that I had finally put all the negativity of my past behind me.

Then I caught the first episode of 'Real Housewives of Atlanta' on the Bravo Television Network. The episode I saw aired on November 28, 2010. It was always my presumption that Phaedra had moved on with her life, distancing herself from her criminal enterprise. I assumed she was now on the straight and narrow. So I was in a total state of shock when I learned that she married Apollo. Apollo was my criminal partner, our criminal partner. As I watched the show, I was about to die. I mean massive heart attack pains ran through my left arm.

I knew damn well that I didn't just see Everett driving them to and from the hospital in Savannah, Georgia when she had the baby. Oh, and please don't let me forget how Everett had everybody featured in the show from the federal halfway house, when the Rolls Royce picked him up for Phaedra and Apollo's wedding. Hold up! Wait a minute…!

"Bi**h you sent a Rolls Royce to pick this man up from the halfway house when my children and I lived in a shelter? What the hell?" I found myself shouting at the television set.

Then I started wondering about my relationship with Phaedra after I was busted. Do you know how many times I called this broad? How many times I had reached out to her? No really. I don't beg, and I don't run behind

anybody, but she should have reached out to me. Why was the entire gang there except me? I know for a fact that I had earned my stripes! Was this real, man? I mean was this sh** actually happening?

Phaedra had not moved on with her life at all. She was still involved with these people which meant she only distanced herself from me. But why only me...? After doing more research, I learned that while Everett Tripodis was in the halfway house, and before he got released from Federal prison, he worked as a paralegal for her law firm. Wait a minute! Now let me get this sh** straight. I'm sorry mama King for cursing, but please just give me this moment.

Okay, so Phaedra was a slick bi**h. I knew this because she taught me how to be smooth. Phaedra married Apollo so he couldn't testify against her, and of course, she masterminded getting his life on track upon his release from prison. She gave Everett, Apollo's street brother, and our partner in crime, a job as a paralegal working for her law firm. She did nothing for my children, or me, but I had sacrificed and lost everything. Didn't I fit into this equation anywhere? What about me? Why didn't she help me?

Check this out right. For those of you that feel like she doesn't owe me anything. I really could care less how you feel or what you think, but for the sake of argument let's consider this for a moment. When she was the ringleader, we had made an agreement, an unwritten contract. The verbal agreement was, if I ever got caught, Phaedra would represent me.

Phaedra Parks didn't do that! Nor did she even try! Phaedra Parks, an attorney who studied law, could truly care less. She knew what was going to happen to me if I ever got caught. Once I was nabbed by the law, she sat back and did nothing. It was one of my hardest lessons in life. There was no honor amongst thieves.

Then I started thinking again, like I always do! I began to play the course of our relationship through my mind over and over again. Things started to finally make sense to me after that. I remembered when I first arrived in Clayton County Jail, when I was pregnant and Phaedra ignored all my calls. I remembered the conversation with Attorney Freeman. That was the only reason she showed up. I believe he forced her to because he didn't want to be involved, so she had no choice.

I remembered my Federal trial when she said it was a conflict of interest. I remembered Everett's lawyer telling Judge Evans that I was the mastermind. I was the fall guy for the entire operation. Phaedra was never ever my friend, and she had a plan for me the moment she met me. Once it dawned on me how I had been played, I cried helplessly. I hadn't cried that much since the death of my mother. She even went to my mother's funeral, and stood over her dead body.

Phaedra stole my moment. That was my moment. I was supposed to be there standing over my mother. Not Phaedra, damn it! As I continued to watch the show week after week, I realized that Phaedra never ever had a

care in the world for my children or for me. She used me, and she had used my life as a stepping-stone for her own personal greed and gain. She's such a greedy bi**h!

Every time the show aired, I was sure to tune in so I could listen closely to her opening statement *"I'm the ultimate southern belle. I always get what I want!"* This was Phaedra's whole demeanor. She believed that everyone and everything served only beneath her. This all opened my eyes and led me to my realization. That was exactly how she viewed me. I was beneath her. I was a dummy, and an ignorant fool that would never realize what hit me. You got me good Phaedra, just like Curtis had gotten my mother!

The more I watched the show, the angrier I became, and the more counseling I needed. I was about to check myself into a mental hospital when I watched the episode of her giving birth to her baby. I couldn't help it. I started having flashbacks, and going to that dark place. I vividly remembered the day I gave birth to my baby, handcuffed to a bed. Phaedra had her family there with all the cameras and the producers of the show there to support her. I had nothing and no one there to support me. This just wasn't fair! Not on any level!

The episode when the forgotten member of Destiny's child strolled into Phaedra's office crying about how she had been to jail, and just wanted to get her life together. Phaedra actually had the audacity to cry. Are you serious right now Phaedra? Then she said she had the golden touch, and promised that young lady she would assist her in getting her life together. Oh my God!

That was just too much for me to handle.

Then there was the episode when she left her baby for the first time to return to work and she cried. How about you walk a day in my shoes, and let's see how many tears you shed? My newborn baby was taken from me moments after she was born, and where were you then Ms. Phaedra Parks?

Ms. King had to console me! Lord, help me, PLEASE! My battle wasn't over... It was years later, and I was still fighting for my life. I had been framed like Roger Rabbit! That was one of my favorite movies as a kid. I watched it over and over, but never once did I imagine that it would happen to me. It was taking everything in my power to keep me from popping up on Phaedra's doorstep. No lie, especially when I thought of her standing in my spot disrespecting my mother's remains. In my mind, it was as if she had walked straight up to the casket, and spat right in my mother's face. When I thought about everything I had lost, everything she had taken from me. That was my breaking point. I couldn't take it! I had to pull myself together and write it out.

Phaedra, I knew you would be reading this book along with millions of other people throughout the world. I want all of you to know that this was not done out of vengeance, but solely based on justice. Justice, the thing that America was founded on, and God said vengeance is His. Enough said.

Phaedra was a genius at creating illusions. She masterminded the perfect crime against the Federal Government, and everybody involved served time in prison, except her. No, she never put a gun to my head. She never made me do anything. I accepted my faults and I paid my debt to society, but what about how she used me, and destroyed my life? At the time of our campaign of crimes, she was a sworn officer of the law. She had taken an oath to uphold a certain standard.

She knew exactly what would happen if I were to ever get caught. Phaedra Parks just didn't care. She had me working during my pregnancies without regards to my children's well being or mine. Phaedra never cared or considered how they would end up. Why would she help everyone rebuild his or her life, but not reach out to help me? My life had been destroyed, and she played a major role in the destruction.

I called her when my children and I were living in the homeless shelter. I reached out to her on several occasions and she never once lifted a finger to help us. I have one question for Phaedra. My mind really remains boggled and I need to know the reason you were at my mother's funeral, when I now know you obviously didn't care?

Well, I shouldn't expect an honest answer, but I know the truth. It was only Phaedra's ploy to make sure I never implicated her in any of the crimes she masterminded. It was a tactic she used to persuade me that she was a true friend and was indeed on my side. But what type of monster finds joy in other people's pain?

I called just about every attorney in the city of Atlanta pleading my case. I knew I could get her in a civil suit, but every attorney claimed that the statute of limitations would hurt my case. I didn't buy that. I knew the truth. All of a sudden that secret society amongst lawyers actually did exist. The one Phaedra told me she would use if I ever got caught. It was meant to only worked for her, and was never intended for me.

I couldn't begin to tell you how many attorneys I took my case to because I wanted to expose Phaedra for who she really was. I even reached out to Goldie Taylor, this time I went in depth about my prior relationship with Phaedra. I told her about this new manuscript I had completed and asked her if she could help me. She explained that she had just attended Phaedra's wedding, and that I would never make it as a writer. Five minutes later, I received a telephone call from Apollo. Goldie must have given my number to him and Phaedra. I had just changed it the day before, and besides my husband, Goldie was the first person I had given my new number.

Apollo was interested in making things 'go away'. Our conversation was short and brief. I felt that if anyone should be calling me, it should be Phaedra Parks! I had no desire to speak with Apollo. He found that out when I hung up in his face. At that moment I started to wonder if Phaedra was the real reason Goldie had dropped me a few years back after she had promised to function as my literary agent.

Shocked but not surprised by Goldie's actions, I kept pressing. A few days later, I spoke with a reputable attorney who was a friend of my great friend. He told me to file a complaint with someone at the state bar of Georgia. I filed a complaint. It was about thirty-three pages long and took them six weeks to arrive at a decision. My complaint was dismissed. They made reference, as everyone else had done, that there was a statute of limitations. Legally there was nothing to be done.

During this time I began receiving prank calls to my home, prank calls from DFACS, claiming that my children were being abused, and threats were being made against my life. I had awakened a sleeping demon. It was on again, the battle of Armageddon, the fight for my life.

Phaedra Parks broke several rules governed by the State Bar of Georgia.

Rule 1.2 Scope of representation: From the website of the State Bar of Georgia, states that: A lawyer shall not counsel a client to engage in conduct that the lawyer knows is criminal or fraudulent, nor knowingly assist a client in such conduct, but a lawyer may discuss the legal consequences of any proposed course of conduct with a client, and may counsel or assist a client to make a good faith effort to determine the validity, scope, meaning or application of the law.

Rule 4.1 Truthfulness in Statements to others: A lawyer is required to be truthful when dealing with others on a client's behalf, but generally has no affirmative duty to inform an opposing party of relevant facts. A misrepresentation can occur if the lawyer incorporates or affirms a statement of another person that the lawyer knows is false. Misrepresentations can also occur by failure to act.

And most profoundly:

Rule 8.4 MISCONDUCT: It shall be a violation of the Georgia Rules of Professional Conduct for a lawyer to:

(1) Violate or attempt to violate the Georgia Rules of Professional Conduct, knowingly assist or induce another to do so, or do so through the acts of another;

(2) be convicted of a felony;

(3) be convicted of a misdemeanor involving moral turpitude where the underlying conduct relates to the lawyer's fitness to practice law;

(4) engage in professional conduct involving dishonesty, fraud, deceit or misrepresentation;

The maximum penalty for a violation of Rule 8.4(a)(1) is the maximum penalty for the specific Rule violated. The maximum penalty for a violation of Rule 8.4(a)(2) through Rule 8.4(c) is disbarment.

In the court of public opinion this would be an open and shut case. Slam dunk, the truth being that obvious. I don't understand and will never understand how a person sworn to uphold the law could be involved in crimi-

nal racketeering schemes which were carried out against the Federal Government and this person continue to practice law in the state.

During the process of completing this book, I dreamed of a huge black snake inside my bedroom wrapped around my ceiling. I was aware the snake was a representation of the enemy that I was fighting. I knew that a snake in my bedroom suggested that this was personal. I couldn't fathom why the snake was above me, and not under my feet where it should be?

Phaedra seemed to be untouchable and all the way above the law. But with this book, I would like to pull that snake down from over my head, and put it under my feet where it belongs. Besides, my mama told me that the only way to kill a snake is by chopping its head off.

In exposing Phaedra Parks for her wickedness, and showing the world just how much of a snake she really was, I have reclaimed my life. Giving life to the disadvantaged children, and helping the world heal was my other goal. The enemy who constantly tried to destroy my life has lost the fight again, but God opens doors that no man can close, and He closes doors that no man can open.

People of the world, the bible tells us that even Satan disguises himself as an angel of light, and to beware of the wolves in sheep's clothing. My story is a true story of betrayal. I have struggled just about my entire life because no one would listen to my words. But right now, the world hears me and now my life has meaning!

"Do not take revenge, my dear friends, but leave room for God's wrath, for it is written: "It is mine to avenge; I will repay," says the Lord."

Romans 12:19 (NIV)

The following pages are original copies of my Federal indictment, my complaint to the state bar, Phaedra Parks' certificate of service, and the arrest record for Johnnie Cabbell. I refuse to remain silent any longer.

ORIGINAL

IN THE UNITED STATES DISTRICT COURT

FOR THE NORTHERN DISTRICT OF GEORGIA

ATLANTA DIVISION

FILED IN OPEN COURT
U.S.D.C. Atlanta

AUG - 9 2005

LUTHER D. THOMAS, Clerk
By: _____ Deputy Clerk

UNITED STATES OF AMERICA

v.

EVERETT JEROME TRIPODIS,
a.k.a. Edward Bourley
a.k.a Melvin Dudley
ANGELA RONAE STANTON
a.k.a. Regina Bunch
a.k.a. Danielle Cato
SHEREE NICOLE STRICKLAND
a.k.a. Nicole Thompson

CRIMINAL INDICTMENT

NO.

1: 05-CR-381

THE GRAND JURY CHARGES THAT:

<u>COUNT ONE</u>

From a date unknown to the Grand Jury, but sometime after on or about August 22, 2003, and not later than on or about December 23, 2003, within the Northern District of Georgia, defendant, EVERETT JEROME TRIPODIS, a.k.a. Mark Bourley, a.k.a. Melvin Dudley, did conceal, store and possess a stolen motor vehicle, that is, a 2002 Mercedes-Benz G500, Vehicle Identification Number, (VIN), WDCYR49E42X131421, knowing the motor vehicle to have been stolen, said vehicle having crossed a state boundary after being stolen, in that the vehicle was stolen in the State

1

of Mississippi and was brought into the State of Georgia, in violation of Title 18, United States Code, Section 2313.

COUNT TWO

Beginning at a date unknown to the grand jury, but not later than the period from on or about December 19, 2003, through on or about December 23, 2003, within the Northern District of Georgia, the defendant, EVERETT JEROME TRIPODIS, a.k.a. Edward Bourley, a.k.a. Melvin Dudley, did knowingly and unlawfully tamper with and alter the Vehicle Identification Number, (VIN), of a motor vehicle, that is, a 2002 Cadillac Escalade having a true VIN 1GYEK63N52R125501, having tampered and altered its VIN to read as 1GYEK63N23R172096, in violation of Title 18, United States Code, Section 511.

2

Lies of a Real Housewife

COUNT THREE

From a date unknown to the Grand Jury, but at least from December 12, 2003, through December 23, 2003, within the Northern District of Georgia, the defendant, EVERETT JEROME TRIPODIS, a.k.a. Edward Bourley, a.k.a. Melvin Dudley, did conceal, store and possess a stolen motor vehicle, that is, a 2002 Porsche 968 Carrera 4S, Vehicle Identification Number, (VIN), WP0AA299X2S621624, knowing the motor vehicle to have been stolen, said vehicle having crossed a state boundary after being stolen, in that the vehicle was stolen in the State of South Carolina and was brought into the State of Georgia, in violation of Title 18, United States Code, Section 2313.

COUNTS FOUR THROUGH ELEVEN

1. Beginning in October 2003, but not later than December 23, 2003, in the Northern District of Georgia and elsewhere, defendants EVERETT JEROME TRIPODIS, a.k.a. Edward Bourley, a.k.a. Melvin Dudley, and ANGELA RONAE STANTON, a.k.a. Regina Bunch, a.k.a. Danielle Cato, aided and abetted by each other and by

3

others known and unknown to the grand jury, knowingly and willfully devised and intended to devise a scheme and artifice to defraud.

OBJECT

2. The object of the scheme and artifice to defraud was to submit false and fraudulent title applications to the State of Ohio and to cause the State of Ohio to issue and mail duplicate titles for existing vehicles.

3. It was further the object of the scheme and artifice to defraud, to use the fraudulently obtained duplicate titles as documentation of ownership for stolen motor vehicles.

4. It was further the object of the scheme and artifice to defraud, to present the duplicate State of Ohio titles to the Georgia Department of Motor Vehicles in order to obtain Georgia titles to facilitate the concealment, registration, transfer and sale of stolen motor vehicles.

4

according to the directions thereon, the following duplicate Ohio

titles:

Count	Ohio Title Number	Duplicate Title for Vehicle	Actual Title Owner
4	# 8200087220	2003 Hummer H2 VIN 5GRGN23U93H122807	Van Devere, Inc. Akron, Ohio
5	# 8100161183	2003 Mercedes Benz M500 VIN 4JGAB75E03A393150	Fifth Third Auto Leasing Trust Dayton, Ohio
6	# 7900589975	2002 Mercedes Benz G500 VIN WDCYR49E42X128602	Marshal Goldman Motor Sales Warrensville Heights, Ohio
7	# 8000224110	2003 Hummer H2 VIN 5GRGN23U23H124933	Van Devere, Inc. Akron, Ohio
8	# 7702871698	2003 Hummer H2 VIN 5GRGN23U13H108612	Spitzer Buick, Inc. Parma, Ohio
9	# 2900671173	2000 Lincoln Navigator VIN 5LMFU28A3YLJ35287	Performance Pontiac-Olds-GMC, Inc. Wooster, Ohio
10	#7602106984	2003 Cadillac Escalade VIN 1GYEK63N23R172096	Marshal Goldman Motor Sales W a r r e n s v i l l e Heights, Ohio
11	# 7602090903	2004 Porsche Cayenne VIN WP1AC29P94LA91828	Fifth Third Leasing Trust Cincinnati, Ohio

All in violation of Title 18, United States Code, Section 1341

and Section 2.

9

ANGELA STANTON

COUNTS TWELVE THROUGH FOURTEEN

1.   Paragraphs 1 through 9 from Counts four through eleven
are realleged and incorporated herein.

2.   From about October 25, 2003, through December 23, 2003,
in the Northern District of Georgia and elsewhere, defendants,
EVERETT JEROME TRIPODIS, a.k.a. Edward Bourley, a.k.a. Melvin
Dudley and ANGELA RONAE STANTON, a.k.a. Regina Bunch, a.k.a.
Danielle Cato, aided and abetted by each other and by others
known and unknown to the grand jury, for the purpose of executing
and attempting to execute the aforementioned scheme and artifice
to defraud, did cause to be placed in the mail applications for
duplicate titles and did direct the Ohio Bureau of Motor Vehicles
to mail duplicate titles to the Northern District of Georgia for
the following vehicles:

Count	Vehicle	Actual Title Owner
12	2003 Chevrolet Tahoe VIN 1GNEK13Zx2J149956	Lariche Used Car Center Findley, Ohio
13	2003 Chevrolet Tahoe VIN 1GNEK13Z93J175725	Jake Sweeney Chevrolet Imports, Inc. Cincinnati, Ohio
14	2003 GMC Yukon Denali VIN 1GKEK63UX3J162030	Jake Sweeney Chevrolet Imports, Cincinnati, Ohio

All in violation of Title 18, United States Code, Section
1341 and Section 2.

10

233

COUNT FIFTEEN

In or about March 2004, but not later than March 3, 2004, within the Northern District of Georgia, defendants, ANGELA RONAE STANTON, a.k.a. Regina Bunch, a.k.a. Danielle Cato, and SHEREE NICOLE STRICKLAND, a.k.a. Nicole Thompson, aided and abetted by each other, knowingly received, possessed and disposed of a falsely made security, that is, a fraudulently obtained Mississippi duplicate title for a 2003 Hummer H2, which moved as, was a part of and constituted interstate commerce, knowing the same to have been falsely made, in violation of Title 18, United States Code, Section 2314 and Section 2.

COUNT SIXTEEN

In or about March 2004, but not later than March 17, 2004, within the Northern District of Georgia, defendants, ANGELA RONAE STANTON, a.k.a. Regina Bunch, a.k.a. Danielle Cato, and SHEREE NICOLE STRICKLAND, a.k.a. Nicole Thompson, aided and abetted by each other, knowingly received, possessed and disposed of a falsely made security, to wit, a fraudulently obtained Tennessee duplicate title for a 2003 Cadillac Escalade, Vehicle Identification Number, (VIN), 1GYEK63N23R118040, which moved as, was a part of and constituted interstate commerce, knowing the same to have been falsely made, in violation of Title 18, United

11

234

Escalade, Vehicle Identification Number, (VIN), 1GYEK63N12R1912219, to Hunt Nissan in Chattanooga, Tennessee.

All in violation of Title 18, United States Code Section 371.

A _____*TRUE*_____ BILL

_____
FOREPERSON

DAVID E. NAHMIAS
UNITED STATES ATTORNEY

JOSEPH A. PLUMMER
ASSISTANT UNITED STATES ATTORNEY
Georgia Bar No. 003006

600 United States Courthouse
75 Spring Street, S.W.
Atlanta, Georgia 30335
Telephone: 404-581-6055

19

STATE BAR OF GEORGIA
GRIEVANCE
CONFIDENTIAL

Please type or print legibly.

YOUR NAME: (Mr./Mrs./Ms.) MS. Angela Stanton

MAILING ADDRESS: 2406 Stone dr. Lilburn, ga 30047
    Street or P. O. Box   City   State   Zip

YOUR PHONE NUMBERS: (W) 404-721-6598   (H) 770-879-0322

NAME OF THE ATTORNEY: Phaedra C. Parks, Esq.
    Fill out a separate form for each attorney. Do not list law firms.

ADDRESS OF THE ATTORNEY: 3575 Piedmont Rd. 15 Piedmont center atl, ga

DATE OF FIRST CONTACT WITH ATTORNEY: 1999   DATE OF LAST CONTACT WITH ATTORNEY: 2006

DOES THIS ATTORNEY CURRENTLY REPRESENT YOU? NO

STATE WHAT THE ATTORNEY HAS DONE OR HAS NOT DONE THAT CAUSES YOU TO SUBMIT THIS REPORT.

See
    attached

"I affirm that the information I have provided here is true to the best of my knowledge."

Return to: State Bar of Georgia
     Office of the General Counsel   SIGNATURE: Angela M. Stanton
     104 Marietta Street, NW
     Suite 100
     Atlanta, Georgia 30303   DATE: 12-15-10

OPTIONAL: PLEASE PROVIDE THE NAME AND PHONE NUMBER OF SOMEONE WE CAN CONTACT IF WE HAVE DIFFICULTY CONTACTING YOU:

NAME OF CONTACT PERSON: Lee Matthews

PHONE NUMBERS OF CONTACT PERSON: (W) 404-914-0040   (H) 770-879-0322

IF YOU HAVE A DISABILITY AND NEED ASSISTANCE IN THE GRIEVANCE PROCESS, PLEASE CONTACT THE ADA COORDINATOR AT (404) 527-8720 OR (800) 334-6865.

I first met Phaedra in 1999 while I was dating Terrance Cook a well named rapper who went by the name of "Drama." Although my relationship with Drama ended quickly; Phaedra and I remained close and in contact with each other. I considered Phaedra as a mentor and I often reached out to her for guidance. A victim of child molestation, I came from a broken family and I was very, very naïve. I was also a single mother of three at the time. I looked up to Phaedra.

In 2000 Phaedra introduced me to her now husband Apollo Nyda. She expressed her concern for my well being and suggested that I work on the side for her as a business partner. (Under the table.) She told me that I would make thousands of dollars and the only thing I had to do was know how to hold a decent conversation and keep my mouth shut if ever questioned by authorities.

2000 was the year that most of the criminal activity began. Phaedra Parks promised me that if I ever got in any trouble she would represent me. Throughout the course of the year I was provided with a computer printout of brand name electronics and model numbers. I then purchased these items with fraudulent checks provided by Phaedra. Lap tops, desk tops, DVD players, palm pilots, jewelry, home furnishings and etc.

I met her each work morning at her home which was located at:

1080 Oregon Trail, Marietta, Georgia

Or either her office she shared with Attorney Ronald Freeman located at:

1069 Spring Street, Atlanta, Georgia

In 2001 0while I was pregnant with my fourth child Phaedra and Apollo both drove me to Hartsfield Atlanta airport and had me go inside to purchase a round trip ticket to Washington, DC

I was provided with fake documents. A bank statement, a utility bill, a social security number print out, and a fraudulent Georgia drivers license all associated with the name Tara Evans. Once I landed in Washington, DC. I was instructed to catch a cab to the Department of Motor Vehicles in Baltimore, MD. I gave the DMV agent the id and the documents she then issued me a MD state drivers license. I returned to Atlanta later that evening. Phaedra picked me up from the airport.

I was then instructed to use that same id and open a bank account at bank of America. That account was open in the summer of 2001 at bank of America located at:

231 Peachtree Street, Atlanta, Georgia

After 30 days Phaedra gave me a check made out to Tara Evans in the amount of $27,000. Ten days later Apollo picked me up and transported me to two different bank of America locations to withdraw the funds. I was given $4000 and we met Phaedra at the Checkers restaurant on Tenth and Spring streets and gave her the remaining $23,000. At this time I was 7 months pregnant.

Phaedra I thought was my friend and my mentor. My children and I were living better. I had my own place, my own vehicle and my best friend was some fancy lawyer. Life was great... at least that's what I thought. Phaedra visited me in the hospital during my childbirth with gifts in arms. She claimed to be the godmother of my baby son Jayvien. Phaedra was considered a family member often visiting my mother and grandmother with or without me, she was always welcome.

Two months after the birth of my son we were back to work. Phaedra informed me that she had another big job for me. This time introducing me to Apollo's street brother Everett

4

Tripodis. I met Everett at Phaedra's office. It was determined that I would be the front man for this operation. A federal racketeering scheme that involved the theft of luxury vehicles. Phaedra provided me with fraudulent Ohio state vehicle titles. I was then given a power of attorney and instructed to go to the DMV office in Hapeville, Georgia and transfer the titles to the name of Danielle Cato. There were so many titles that the task became overwhelming. Phaedra insisted that I enlist the help of my cousin Sheree Strickland. Sheree was paid $300 for each title she transferred. In the meantime I was sent out to luxury car lots to scope out vehicles by maintain the VIN number. I would then report back to Phaedra or Everett the recorded numbers.

Sometimes the same day or the day after I would receive a fraudulent registration card along with an identification card. I would take those items to another luxury dealership and tell them I lost my key. They would then charge $185 for another computerized cut key. Those keys were used to later steel those vehicles off of the lot after the dealership closed for the day.

Once the cars were completely flipped they were driven out of state and traded in for vehicles of lesser value. We walked away with a different vehicle and checks no lesser than $20,000 an elaborate scheme that worked.

In March of 2004, while I was seven months pregnant with my 5th child, things went sour. Me and Everett both were arrested in Chattanooga, Tennessee at a car dealership. I was finally extradited back to Clayton County Georgia where I faced state charges for title fraud. I continuously called Phaedra along with my mother, father, brother and grandmother to no avail. I had my cousin Calvin Milling call Ronald Freeman's office on a 3way call from Clayton county jail. I talked with Ronald Freeman personally. He was in fact fully aware of the illegal transactions that took place between Phaedra and myself.

I explained to him my disgust with Phaedra. Her acting as if everything was alright and nothing was going on! I was getting closer to my due date and it didn't seem as if she was going to help me. I suggested that he have a talk with Phaedra in regards to our verbal agreement that she was to represent me, because if she didn't there was no telling which way this case would blow and he could find himself implicated. 5 minutes later Phaedra was on the phone. Calvin Milling will bear witness to this conversation.

IN THE SUPERIOR COURT OF CLAYTON COUNTY
STATE OF GEORGIA

FILED
CLAYTON CO., GA.
2004 JUL 26 PM 1:47
LINDA T. MILLER
CLERK SUPERIOR COURT

The State of Georgia	:
	:
	:
v.	: Case No.: 2002-CR-00413-8
	:
Angela Ronae Stanton,	:
	:
Defendant.	:

CERTIFICATE OF SERVICE

I hereby certify that I have this day served the District Attorney of Clayton County (or one of

his assistants) with a true and accurate copy of the within and foregoing **MOTION TO MODIFY**

SENTENCE by U.S. Mail with adequate postage.

Elliot Spencer, II- P.O.II
Robert E. Keller, District Attorney
Clayton County District Attorney Office
Harold R. Banke Justice Center, 9157 Tara Blvd
Jonesboro, Georgia 30236

This _23rd_ day of July, 2004.

PHAEDRA C. PARKS
Georgia Bar No. 556388
Attorney for Defendant Angela Stanton

THE PARKS GROUP
1069 Spring Street, N.W.
Atlanta, Georgia 30309-3817
(404) 873-0093
(404) 873-1103 (Facsimile)

	AGENCY ID. (ORI)		**INCIDENT REPORT**			CASE NUMBER
8A	GA GA0440200					08-076022

EVENT

INCIDENT TYPE			COUNTS	INCIDENT CODE		PREMISE TYPE			
RAPE - STRONGARM			1	1103		1 HIGHWAY	2 SVC. STATION		
EXECUTED SEARCH WARRANT			1	7399		3 CONVENIENCE STORE	4 BANK		
						5 COMMERCIAL	V RESIDENCE		
						7 SCHOOL CAMPUS	8 ALL OTHER		

INCIDENT LOCATION				LOC CODE			WEAPON TYPE		
4390 CREEK BEND CIR CONLEY GA				371					

INCIDENT DATE	TIME	DATE	TIME	STRANGER TO STRANGER	GUN	WEAPON TYPE	
06/07/2008	15:45	TO 06/07/2008	18:15	YES NO V UNK	1 GUN	2 KNIFE CUTTING TOOL	
					IV HANDS/FIST, ECT.	4 OTHER	

COMPLAINANT	ADDRESS		PHONE NUMBER
STANTON, ANGELA RONAE			

VICTIM

VICTIM'S NAME		RACE	SEX	AGE	RESIDENCE PHONE		BUSINESS PHONE
STANTON, ANGELA RONAE		B	F	37			

ADDRESS		CENSUS TRACT	EMPLOYER OR OCCUPATION	
			UNKNOWN OR NOT STATED	

STUDENT? YES V NO	IF YES, NAME VICTIM'S SCHOOL		

OFFENDER

NAME		RACE	SEX	DATE OF BIRTH	AGE
CABBELL, JOHNNIE JR.		B	M	01/18/1974	32

WANTED	ADDRESS	CENSUS TRACT	HEIGHT	WEIGHT	HAIR	EYES
	4390 CREEK BEND CIR CONLEY GA 30288-	600	270	1 BLACK	2 BROWN

WARRANT	CHARGES	COUNTS	OFFENSE CODE	OFFENSE/ARREST	JURIS.
	RAPE - STRONGARM	1	1103	2	1. CITY
ARREST	ALL OTHER OFFENSES	1	7399	2	2. COUNTY
V					3. STATE
					4. OUT OF STATE
					5. UNKNOWN

TOTAL NUMBER ARRESTED	ARREST AT OR NEAR OFFENSE SCENE	DATE OF OFFENSE
	YES NO V	06/07/2008

VEHICLE

	TAG NUMBER	STATE	YEAR	V.I.N.
STOLEN				
RECOVD	YEAR	MAKE	MODEL	STYLE	COLOR
SUSPECTS					

	MOTOR SIZE (CID)	AUTO	MAN.	INSURED BY
		TRANS		

WITNESS

NAMES	ADDRESS	PHONE NUMBER

PROPERTY

	VEHICLES	CURRENCY, NOTES, ETC	JEWELRY, PREC. METALS	FURS	PROPERTY RECOVERY INFO ONLY	
STOLEN					THEFT/RECOVERY	JURISDICTION CODES
RECOVERED						1. CITY
	CLOTHING	OFFICE EQUIP.	TV, RADIO, ETC	HOUSEHOLD GOODS		2. COUNTY
STOLEN					DATE OF THEFT	3. STATE
RECOVERED						4. OUT OF STATE
	FIREARMS	CONSUMABLE GOODS	LIVESTOCK	OTHER	TOTAL	5. UNKNOWN
STOLEN						
RECOVERED						

ADM

GCIC ENTRY	WARRANT	MISSING PERSONS	VEHICLE	ARTICLE	BOAT	GUN	SECURITIES

DRUG

DID INVESTIGATION INDICATE THAT THIS INCIDENT WAS DRUG-RELATED?	YES	V NO		
IF YES, PLEASE INDICATE THE TYPE OF DRUG(S) USED BY OFFENDER				
1 - AMPHETAMINE	2 - BARBITURATE	3 - COCAINE	4 - HALLUCINOGEN	5 - HEROIN
6 - MARIJUANA	7 - METHAMPHETAMINE	8 - OPIUM	9 - SYNTHETIC NARCOTIC	U - UNKNOWN

CLEAR

REQUIRED DATA FIELDS FOR CLEARANCE REPORT	CLEARED BY ARREST	V EXCEPTIONALLY CLEARED	UNFOUNDED	REPORT DATE 06/07/2008
DATE OF CLEARANCE 06/07/2008	V ADULT	JUVENILE		

NARRATIVE

****

Narrative Title: INITIAL REPORT
Date Entered: 6/7/2008 11:35:25 PM

REPORTING OFFICER	NUMBER	APPROVING OFFICER	NUMBER
T C MACK	2330		

GCIC-UCR-004
(5/92)

www.dontaskjusttell.org

Silence destroys lives. So please Don't Ask
Just Tell, and Stop the silence!

THE *Hood* IS MOBILE...

AUGUSTUS PUBLISHING

WHERE **HIP HOP LITERATURE** BEGINS

LOVE & A GANGSTA
ERICK S GRAY

UNBELIEVABLE: THE LIFE DEATH AND AFTER LIFE OF THE NOTORIOUS B.I.G
CHEO HODARI COKER

HARD WHITE
SHANNON HOLMES

SCAN HERE: READ AN EXCEPT
AND WATCH A BOOK TRAILER

AUGUSTUSPUBLISHING.COM

FOR BOOK STORE ORDERS CONTACT: PUBLISHERS GROUP WEST
WWW.PGW.COM | CUSTOMER SERVICE 800-788-3123

nook
by Barnes & Noble

amazonkindle

Our titles interlace action, crime, and the urban lifestyle depicting the harsh realities of life on the streets. Call it street literature, urban drama, we call it hip-hop literature. This exciting genre features fast-paced action, gritty ghetto realism, and social messages about the high price of the street life style.

DEAD AND STINKIN'
STEPHEN HEWETT

A GOOD DAY TO DIE
JAMES HENDRICKS

WHEN LOVE TURNS TO HATE
SHARRON DOYLE

IF IT AIN'T ONE THING IT'S ANOTHER
SHARRON DOYLE

WOMAN'S CRY
VANESSA MARTIR

BLACKOUT
JERRY LaMOTHE
ANTHONY WHYTE

HUSTLE HARD
BLAINE MARTIN

A BOOGIE DOWN STORY
KEISHA SEIGNIOUS

CRAVE ALL LOSE ALL
ERICK S GRAY

LOVE AND A GANGSTA
ERICK S GRAY

LOVE AND A GANGSTA
ERICK S GRAY

LOVE AND A GANGSTA
ERICK S GRAY

Mail us a List of the titles you would like include $14.95 per Title + shipping charges $3.95 for one book & $1.00 for each additional book. Make all checks payable to: Augustus Publishing 33 Indian Rd. NY, NY 10034

HARD WHITE
SHANNON HOLMES
ANTHONY WHYTE

STREET CHIC
ANTHONY WHYTE

CRAVE ALL LOSE ALL
ERICK S GRAY

LOVE & A GANGSTA
ERICK S GRAY

STREETS OF NEW YORK VOL. 1
ERICK S GRAY, ANTHONY WHYTE
MARK ANTHONY, SHANNON HOLMES

STREETS OF NEW YORK VOL. 2
ERICK S GRAY, ANTHONY WHYTE
MARK ANTHONY, K'WAN

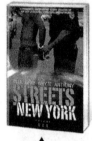

STREETS OF NEW YORK VOL. 2
ERICK S GRAY, ANTHONY WHYTE
MARK ANTHONY, TREASURE BLUE

SMUT CENTRAL
BRANDON McCALLA

GHETTO GIRLS
ANTHONY WHYTE

GHETTO GIRLS TOO
ANTHONY WHYTE

GHETTO GIRLS 3:
SOO HOOD
ANTHONY WHYTE

GHETTO GIRLS IV:
YOUNG LUV
ANTHONY WHYTE

SPOT RUSHERS
BRANDON McCALLA

IT CAN HAPPEN
IN A MINUTE
S.M. JOHNSON

LIPSTICK DIARIES
CRYSTAL LACEY WINSLOW
VARIOUS FEMALE AUTHORS

LIPSTICK DIARIES 2
WAHIDA CLARK
VARIOUS FEMALE AUTHORS

CPSIA information can be obtained
at www.ICGtesting.com
Printed in the USA
LVOW03s1147300717
543058LV00001B/1/P